Presented

to

Big Steve
_____

by

Lumpy
_____

5/2/03
_____
Date

Love
ya!

TABLE OF CONTENTS

TABLE OF CONTENTS

TABLE OF CONTENTS

TABLE OF CONTENTS

Unless otherwise indicated, all Scripture quotations are taken from the King James Version of the Bible.

One-Minute Pocket Bible For Fathers
ISBN 1-56394-019-1/B-51
Copyright © 1994 by *MIKE MURDOCK*
All publishing rights belong exclusively to Wisdom International
Published by The Wisdom Center
P. O. Box 99 • Denton, Texas 76202
1-888-WISDOM-1 (1-888-947-3661)
Website: www.thewisdomcenter.tv

FACTS ABOUT FATHERS

It has been said that "A child is not likely to find a father in God unless he finds something of God in his father." Being a father is indeed a sacred privilege. At the same time it can be a struggle and a challenge.

As a Christian father, you have to continually go back over and straighten out the daily influence of a degenerative society on your child. No matter how diligent and careful you are, your child will most probably be bombarded with negative, undesirable factors. Still, you have God's promise of security. Proverbs 22:6 tells us to, "Train up a child in the way he should go: and when he is old, he will not depart from it."

A father will do his best to instill Godly character in his child and then trust the Everlasting Father to complete the work. He is a man of honesty and integrity. A true father is not afraid to laugh or cry, to admit his mistakes, to be tender and loving, even when he is weary. Spiritually, he will teach his children the laws and precepts of God and make his home a natural dwelling place for the presence of the Lord. There are great rewards for this tender warrior. Proverbs 23:24 states, "The father of the righteous shall greatly rejoice: and he that begetteth a wise child shall have joy for him."

The importance of the first years of your child's life cannot be stressed enough. Someone has said that 50 percent of a child's character is formed by the age of two. Eighty percent of his character is developed by the age of five. You can provide a constant source of love and attention for your child. At the same time, no one can provide a sense of Wisdom, authority and security like a father. You need to be a nurturer even as it is inherently natural for a mother. Your expression of emotions adds depth and richness to your child's personality.

In years past, the family unit consisted of a mother and father. Today, unfortunately, one-third of our kids do not live with their natural fathers. Over fifteen million children grow up in homes without any father. And throughout most of the 1970s and 80s, one million kids a year watched their parents split up, (*Newsweek,* January 13, 1992). If you fall in this category, you face an even greater challenge than the father who is allowed daily input into his child's life.

The primary values, attitudes and skills that your children possess will be obtained through your influence. There is no great formula for being a good father, but you have a great example in your Heavenly Father. You would do well to study His character and attributes to understand how to father effectively. I have listed below some of His traits that are available to you as a father.

31 Qualities Of Your Heavenly Father

1. **Your Heavenly Father Is**

Love. "Yea, I have loved thee with an everlasting love:" *(Jeremiah 31:3)*

2. **Your Heavenly Father Is Present.** "Whither shall I go from Thy Spirit? or whither shall I flee from Thy presence?" *(Psalm 139:7)*

3. **Your Heavenly Father Is Holy.** "Sanctify yourselves therefore, and be ye holy: for I am the Lord your God." *(Leviticus 20:7)*

4. **Your Heavenly Father Is Reliable.** "God is not a man, that He should lie; neither the son of man, that He should repent: hath He said, and shall He not do it? or hath He spoken, and shall He not make it good?" *(Numbers 23:19)*

5. **Your Heavenly Father Is Strong.** "I will trust, and not be afraid: for the Lord Jehovah is my strength." *(Isaiah 12:2)*

6. **Your Heavenly Father Is Wise.** "And the Spirit of the Lord shall rest upon him, the Spirit of wisdom and understanding," *(Isaiah 11:2)*

7. **Your Heavenly Father Is Available.** "The Lord is nigh unto all them that call upon Him," *(Psalm 145:18)*

8. **Your Heavenly Father Is Creative.** "For thus saith the Lord that created the heavens; God Himself that formed the earth and made it;" *(Isaiah 45:18)*

9. **Your Heavenly Father Is Steadfast.** "Be strong and of a good courage, Fear not, nor be afraid of them: for the Lord Thy God, He it is that doth go with thee; He will not fail thee, nor forsake

thee." *(Deuteronomy 31:6)*

10. **Your Heavenly Father Is Generous.** "The Lord shall increase you more and more, you and your children." *(Psalm 115:14)*

11. **Your Heavenly Father Is Just.** "Touching the Almighty, we cannot find Him out: He is excellent in power, and in judgement, and in plenty of justice:" *(Job 37:23)*

12. **Your Heavenly Father Is Kind.** "For His merciful kindness is great toward us:" *(Psalm 117:2)*

13. **Your Heavenly Father Is Responsive.** "Then shalt thou call, and the Lord shall answer; thou shalt cry, and He shall say, Here I am." *(Isaiah 58:9)*

14. **Your Heavenly Father Is Forgiving.** "For Thou, Lord, art good, and ready to forgive; and plenteous in mercy unto all them that call upon Thee." *(Psalm 86:5)*

15. **Your Heavenly Father Is Faithful.** "Thy faithfulness is unto all generations:" *(Psalm 119:90)*

16. **Your Heavenly Father Is Secure.** "And I give unto them eternal life; and they shall never perish, neither shall any man pluck them out of My hand." *(John 10:28)*

17. **Your Heavenly Father Is Peaceful.** "The Lord will bless His people with peace." *(Psalm 29:11)*

18. **Your Heavenly Father Is Joyful.** "These things have I spoken unto you, that My joy might remain in you, and that your joy might be full." *(John 15:11)*

19. **Your Heavenly Father Is Righteous.** "Thy righteousness is like the great mountains;" *(Psalm 36:6)*

20. **Your Heavenly Father Is Merciful.** "Great are Thy tender mercies, O Lord:" *(Psalm 119:156)*

21. **Your Heavenly Father Is Stable.** "The Lord is my rock, and my fortress, and my deliverer; my God, my strength, in Whom I will trust; my buckler, and the horn of my salvation, and my high tower." *(Psalm 18:2)*

22. **Your Heavenly Father Is Accessible.** "Come unto Me, all ye that labour and are heavy laden, and I will give you rest." *(Matthew 11:28)*

23. **Your Heavenly Father Is Truthful.** "For the Lord is good; His mercy is everlasting; and His truth endureth to all generations." *(Psalm 100:5)*

24. **Your Heavenly Father Is Patient.** "But Thou, O Lord, art a God full of compassion, and gracious, longsuffering, and plenteous in mercy and truth." *(Psalm 86:15)*

25. **Your Heavenly Father Is Gracious.** "Gracious is the Lord, and righteous;" *(Psalm 116:5)*

26. **Your Heavenly Father Is A Finisher.** "Thus the heavens and the earth were finished, and all the host of them." *(Genesis 2:1)*

27. **Your Heavenly Father Is Goal-Oriented.** "For the Son of man is come to seek and to save that which was lost." *(Luke 19:10)*

28. **Your Heavenly Father Is A**

Listener. "For by thy words thou shalt be justified, and by thy words thou shalt be condemned." *(Matthew 12:37)*

29. **Your Heavenly Father Is A Planner.** "In My Father's house are many mansions: if it were not so, I would have told you. I go to prepare a place for you." *(John 14:2)*

30. **Your Heavenly Father Is A Problem-Solver.** "How God anointed Jesus of Nazareth with the Holy Ghost and with power: Who went about doing good, and healing all that were oppressed of the devil; for God was with Him." *(Acts 10:38)*

31. **Your Heavenly Father Is A Safe Harbor.** "For Thou hast been a shelter for me, and a strong tower from the enemy." *(Psalm 61:3)*

Earlier I said there were no formulas for becoming a good father. After going through this list, I admit I was wrong. The Scriptures provide the greatest pattern possible for being a good father. What is exciting is that each of these attributes is totally possible for the Christian father today.

God bless you Father! Remember to "...seek ye first the kingdom of God, and His righteousness; and all these things shall be added unto you" (Matthew 6:33). And in those times when you feel overwhelmed and inadequate, remember to: "Trust in the Lord with all thine heart; and lean not unto thine own understanding" (Proverbs 3:5).

A Father's Prayer

My Dear Heavenly Father,

Thank You for being accessible to me.

Sensitive to my desires.

Tender toward my wounds.

Concerned about my responsibilities.

I, too, am a father. So I know You understand me. Sometimes I love being a father. Sometimes it is a burden I do not know how to carry.

Please help me to hear Your voice, obey Your instructions and be the father that pleases Your heart, even when my family is not happy with my decisions.

Thank You for children who are truly the heritage of the Lord and the companion that You have assigned to me.

Your Word has been my only consistent hope, the only thing that has never changed in my life, and the only promise my heart is capable of believing.

I embrace Your Wisdom every single day of my life.

In Jesus' Name...Amen.

ABILITIES

For the Lord shall be thy confidence,
Proverbs 3:26

Not by might, nor by power, but by My
spirit, saith the Lord of hosts.
Zechariah 4:6

Verily, verily, I say unto you, He that
believeth on Me, the works that I do shall
he do also; and greater works than these
shall he do; because I go unto My Father.
John 14:12

What shall we then say to these
things? If God be for us, who can be against
us? *Romans 8:31*

For the gifts and calling of God are
without repentance. *Romans 11:29*

But we have the mind of Christ.
1 Corinthians 2:16

And let us not be weary in well doing:
for in due season we shall reap, if we faint
not. *Galatians 6:9*

I can do all things through Christ
which strengtheneth me. *Philippians 4:13*

**NOTHING IS EVER AS DIFFICULT
AS IT FIRST APPEARS.**
-MIKE MURDOCK

ACHIEVEMENT

Lord, all my desire is before Thee;
Psalm 38:9

The soul of the sluggard desireth, and hath nothing: but the soul of the diligent shall be made fat. *Proverbs 13:4*

So shall My word be that goeth forth out of My mouth: it shall not return unto Me void, but it shall accomplish that which I please, and it shall prosper in the thing whereto I sent it. *Isaiah 55:11*

The Lord is good unto them that wait for Him, to the soul that seeketh Him.
Lamentations 3:25

Therefore I say unto you, What things soever ye desire, when ye pray, believe that ye receive them, and ye shall have them.
Mark 11:24

But without faith it is impossible to please Him; for he that cometh to God must believe that He is, and that He is a rewarder of them that diligently seek Him.
Hebrews 11:6

EVERY CREATION CONTAINS AN INVISIBLE COMMAND FROM GOD TO MULTIPLY AND BECOME MORE.
-MIKE MURDOCK

APPEARANCE

But the Lord said unto Samuel, Look not on his countenance, or on the height of his stature; because I have refused him: for the Lord seeth not as man seeth; for man looketh on the outward appearance, but the Lord looketh on the heart.
1 Samuel 16:7

For the Lord taketh pleasure in His people: He will beautify the meek with salvation. *Psalm 149:4*

A merry heart maketh a cheerful countenance: but by sorrow of the heart the spirit is broken. *Proverbs 15:13*

Do ye look on things after the outward appearance? If any man trust to himself that he is Christ's, let him of himself think this again, that, as he is Christ's, even so are we Christ's. *2 Corinthians 10:7*

Whose adorning let it not be that outward adorning of plaiting the hair, and of wearing of gold, or of putting on of apparel; But let it be the hidden man of the heart, in that which is not corruptible, even the ornament of a meek and quiet spirit, which is in the sight of God of great price. *1 Peter 3:3,4*

PEOPLE SEE WHAT YOU ARE BEFORE THEY HEAR WHAT YOU ARE.
-MIKE MURDOCK

ASSIGNMENT

For promotion cometh neither from the east, nor from the west, nor from the south. But God is the judge: He putteth down one, and setteth up another.

Psalm 75:6,7

And let the beauty of the Lord our God be upon us: and establish thou the work of our hands upon us; yea, the work of our hands establish Thou it.

Psalm 90:17

Seest thou a man diligent in his business? he shall stand before kings; he shall not stand before mean men.

Proverbs 22:29

And thine ears shall hear a word behind thee, saying, This is the way, walk ye in it, when ye turn to the right hand, and when ye turn to the left.   *Isaiah 30:21*

Let every man abide in the same calling wherein he was called.

1 Corinthians 7:20

YOUR ASSIGNMENT IS DECIDED BY GOD AND DISCOVERED BY YOU. IT IS GEOGRAPHICAL AND IS ALWAYS TO A PERSON OR PEOPLE. IT IS ALWAYS TO SOLVE A PROBLEM FOR SOMEONE.

-MIKE MURDOCK

ATTITUDE

Teach me, and I will hold my tongue: and cause me to understand wherein I have erred.   *Job 6:24*

For out of the abundance of the heart the mouth speaketh. But I say unto you, That every idle word that men shall speak, they shall give account thereof in the day of judgment. For by thy words thou shalt be justified, and by thy words thou shalt be condemned.   *Matthew 12:34,36,37*

Be ye angry, and sin not: let not the sun go down upon your wrath:
                    Ephesians 4:26

Let your conversation be without covetousness; and be content with such things as ye have: for He hath said, I will never leave thee, nor forsake thee.
                    Hebrews 13:5

Grudge not one against another, brethren, lest ye be condemned: behold, the judge standeth before the door.
                    James 5:9

YOUR ATTITUDE DETERMINES THE SEASON YOU ENTER.
                    -MIKE MURDOCK

BIBLE

Ye shall not add unto the word which I command you, neither shall ye diminish ought from it, that ye may keep the commandments of the Lord your God which I command you.   *Deuteronomy 4:2*

The law of the Lord is perfect, converting the soul: the testimony of the Lord is sure, making wise the simple.
Psalm 19:7

Thy word have I hid in mine heart, that I might not sin against Thee. Thy word is a lamp unto my feet, and a light unto my path.   *Psalm 119:11,105*

Heaven and earth shall pass away: but My words shall not pass away.
Mark 13:31

All scripture is given by inspiration of God, and is profitable for doctrine, for reproof, for correction, for instruction in righteousness: That the man of God may be perfect, throughly furnished unto all good works.   *2 Timothy 3:16,17*

For the word of God is quick, and powerful, and sharper than any twoedged sword, piercing even to the dividing asunder of soul and spirit, and of the joints and marrow, and is a discerner of the thoughts and intents of the heart.
Hebrews 4:12

GOD'S ONLY NEED IS TO BE BELIEVED.
HIS ONLY PAIN IS TO BE DOUBTED.
-MIKE MURDOCK

BUSINESS

Go to the ant, thou sluggard; consider her ways, and be wise: Which having no guide, overseer, or ruler, Provideth her meat in the summer, and gathereth her food in the harvest. *Proverbs 6:6-8*

Seest thou a man diligent in his business? he shall stand before kings; he shall not stand before mean men.
Proverbs 22:29

He that tilleth his land shall have plenty of bread: but he that followeth after vain persons shall have poverty enough.
Proverbs 28:19

When I applied mine heart to know wisdom, and to see the business that is done upon the earth: for also there is that neither day nor night seeth sleep with his eyes: *Ecclesiastes 8:16*

Not slothful in business; fervent in spirit; serving the Lord; Rejoicing in hope; patient in tribulation; continuing instant in prayer; *Romans 12:11,12*

And that ye study to be quiet, and to do your own business, and to work with your own hands, as we commanded you;
1 Thessalonians 4:11

> **IF GOD IS YOUR PARTNER YOU CAN AFFORD TO MAKE BIG PLANS.**
> *-MIKE MURDOCK*

CHARACTER

Blessed is the man that walketh not in the counsel of the ungodly, nor standeth in the way of sinners, nor sitteth in the seat of the scornful. But his delight is in the law of the Lord; and in His law doth he meditate day and night.   *Psalm 1:1,2*

Let integrity and uprightness preserve me; for I wait on thee.   *Psalm 25:21*

Judge me, O Lord; for I have walked in mine integrity: I have trusted also in the Lord; therefore I shall not slide.
     Psalm 26:1

And as for me, thou upholdest me in mine integrity, and settest me before thy face for ever.   *Psalm 41:12*

Recompense to no man evil for evil. Provide things honest in the sight of all men. If it be possible, as much as lieth in you, live peaceably with all men.
     Romans 12:17,18

Finally, brethren, whatsoever things are true, whatsoever things are honest, whatsoever things are just, whatsoever things are pure, whatsoever things are lovely, whatsoever things are of good report; if there be any virtue, and if there be any praise, think on these things.
     Philippians 4:8

YOU CANNOT BE WHAT YOU ARE NOT, BUT YOU CAN BECOME WHAT YOU ARE NOT.
-MIKE MURDOCK

CHURCH ATTENDANCE

And let them make Me a sanctuary;
that I may dwell among them.
Exodus 25:8

One thing have I desired of the Lord,
that will I seek after; that I may dwell in
the house of the Lord all the days of my
life, to behold the beauty of the Lord, and
to enquire in His temple.   *Psalm 27:4*

I was glad when they said unto me,
Let us go into the house of the Lord.
Psalm 122:1

Keep thy foot when thou goest to the
house of God, and be more ready to hear,
than to give the sacrifice of fools: for they
consider not that they do evil.
Ecclesiastes 5:1

For where two or three are gathered
together in My name, there am I in the
midst of them.   *Matthew 18:20*

Not forsaking the assembling of
ourselves together, as the manner of some
is; but exhorting one another: and so much
the more, as ye see the day approaching.
Hebrews 10:25

**CLIMATE DETERMINES
WHAT GROWS WITHIN YOU.**
-MIKE MURDOCK

COMMITMENT

Commit thy way unto the Lord; trust also in Him; and He shall bring it to pass.
Psalm 37:5

Commit thy works unto the Lord, and thy thoughts shall be established.
Proverbs 16:3

He staggered not at the promise of God through unbelief; but was strong in faith, giving glory to God; And being fully persuaded that, what He had promised, He was able also to perform.
Romans 4:20,21

And let us not be weary in well doing: for in due season we shall reap, if we faint not.
Galatians 6:9

Brethren, I count not myself to have apprehended: but this one thing I do, forgetting those things which are behind, and reaching forth unto those things which are before, I press toward the mark for the prize of the high calling of God in Christ Jesus.
Philippians 3:13,14

COMMITMENT IS YOUR DECISION TO MEET THE NEEDS OF THE ONES GOD HAS CALLED YOU TO SERVE.
-MIKE MURDOCK

Communication

And thine ears shall hear a word behind thee, saying, This is the way, walk ye in it, when ye turn to the right hand, and when ye turn to the left.

Isaiah 30:21

Be not deceived: evil communications corrupt good manners.

1 Corinthians 15:33

Let him that is taught in the word communicate unto him that teacheth in all good things. *Galatians 6:6*

Let no corrupt communication proceed out of your mouth, but that which is good to the use of edifying, that it may minister grace unto the hearers.

Ephesians 4:29

Notwithstanding ye have well done, that ye did communicate with my affliction. *Philippians 4:14*

But now ye also put off all these; anger, wrath, malice, blasphemy, filthy communication out of your mouth.

Colossians 3:8

If What You Say To Someone Cannot Be Said To Everyone, Then Say It To No One!

-J.E. MURDOCK

COMPASSION

But He, being full of compassion, forgave their iniquity, and destroyed them not: yea, many a time turned He His anger away, and did not stir up all His wrath.
Psalm 78:38

Unto the upright there ariseth light in the darkness: He is gracious, and full of compassion, and righteous. *Psalm 112:4*

Can a woman forget her sucking child, that she should not have compassion on the son of her womb? yea, they may forget, yet will I not forget thee. *Isaiah 49:15*

And Jesus, when He came out, saw much people, and was moved with compassion toward them, because they were as sheep not having a shepherd: and He began to teach them many things.
Mark 6:34

Finally, be ye all of one mind, having compassion one of another, love as brethren, be pitiful, be courteous:
1 Peter 3:8

THOSE WHO UNLOCK YOUR
COMPASSION ARE THOSE TO WHOM
YOU HAVE BEEN ASSIGNED.
-MIKE MURDOCK

COURAGE

Be strong and of a good courage, fear not, nor be afraid of them: for the Lord thy God, He it is that doth go with thee; He will not fail thee, nor forsake thee.
Deuteronomy 31:6

Have not I commanded thee? Be strong and of a good courage; be not afraid, neither be thou dismayed: for the Lord thy God is with thee whithersoever thou goest.
Joshua 1:9

Be of good courage, and He shall strengthen your heart, all ye that hope in the Lord. *Psalm 31:24*

There shall no evil befall thee, neither shall any plague come nigh thy dwelling.
Psalm 91:10

Strengthen ye the weak hands, and confirm the feeble knees. *Isaiah 35:3*

Fear thou not; for I am with thee: be not dismayed; for I am thy God: I will strengthen thee; yea, I will help thee; yea, I will uphold thee with the right hand of My righteousness. *Isaiah 41:10*

I can do all things through Christ which strengtheneth me. *Philippians 4:13*

WINNERS ARE JUST EX -LOSERS
WHO GOT MAD.
-MIKE MURDOCK

CRISIS

Yea, though I walk through the valley of the shadow of death, I will fear no evil: for Thou art with me; Thy rod and Thy staff they comfort me. *Psalm 23:4*

For in the time of trouble He shall hide me in His pavilion: in the secret of His tabernacle shall He hide me; He shall set me up upon a rock. *Psalm 27:5*

My soul shall make her boast in the Lord: the humble shall hear thereof, and be glad. O magnify the Lord with me, and let us exalt His name together. I sought the Lord, and He heard me, and delivered me from all my fears. *Psalm 34:2-4*

God is our refuge and strength, a very present help in trouble. Therefore will not we fear, though the earth be removed, and though the mountains be carried into the midst of the sea; Though the waters thereof roar and be troubled, though the mountains shake with the swelling thereof. *Psalm 46:1-3*

I will not leave you comfortless: I will come to you. *John 14:18*

> **CRISIS ALWAYS OCCURS AT THE CURVE OF CHANGE.**
> *-MIKE MURDOCK*

CRITICISM

A soft answer turneth away wrath: but grievous words stir up anger.
Proverbs 15:1

Blessed are ye, when men shall revile you, and persecute you, and shall say all manner of evil against you falsely, for My sake. *Matthew 5:11*

But I say unto you, Love your enemies, bless them that curse you, do good to them that hate you, and pray for them which despitefully use you, and persecute you;
Matthew 5:44

And the soldiers likewise demanded of Him, saying, And what shall we do? And He said unto them, Do violence to no man, neither accuse any falsely; and be content with your wages. *Luke 3:14*

But love ye your enemies, and do good, and lend, hoping for nothing again; and your reward shall be great, and ye shall be the children of the Highest: for He is kind unto the unthankful and to the evil.
Luke 6:35

Having a good conscience; that, whereas they speak evil of you, as of evildoers, they may be ashamed that falsely accuse your good conversation in Christ. *1 Peter 3:16*

NEVER SPEND MORE TIME ON A CRITIC THAN YOU WOULD GIVE TO A FRIEND.
-MIKE MURDOCK

DEBT

Thou shalt not borrow.
Deuteronomy 28:12

The wicked borroweth, and payeth not again: but the righteous sheweth mercy, and giveth. *Psalm 37:21*

He that is surety for a stranger shall smart for it: and he that hateth suretyship is sure. *Proverbs 11:15*

The rich ruleth over the poor, and the borrower is servant to the lender.
Proverbs 22:7

Give, and it shall be given unto you; good measure, pressed down, and shaken together, and running over, shall men give into your bosom. For with the same measure that ye mete withal it shall be measured to you again. *Luke 6:38*

Owe no man any thing, but to love one another: *Romans 13:8*

Beloved, I wish above all things that thou mayest prosper and be in health, even as thy soul prospereth. *3 John 1:2*

**DEBT IS PROOF OF GREED.
IT IS THE OPPOSITE OF GIVING.
DEBT IS EMPTYING YOUR FUTURE
TO FILL UP YOUR PRESENT.
GIVING IS EMPTYING YOUR PRESENT
TO FILL UP YOUR FUTURE.**
-MIKE MURDOCK

DECISION-MAKING

And if it seem evil unto you to serve the Lord, choose you this day whom ye will serve; whether the gods which your fathers served that were on the other side of the flood, or the gods of the Amorites, in whose land ye dwell: but as for me and my house, we will serve the Lord.   *Joshua 24:15*

Trust in the Lord with all thine heart; and lean not unto thine own understanding. In all thy ways acknowledge Him, and He shall direct thy paths.   *Proverbs 3:5,6*

He that handleth a matter wisely shall find good: and whoso trusteth in the Lord, happy is he.   *Proverbs 16:20*

But Daniel purposed in his heart that he would not defile himself with the portion of the king's meat, nor with the wine which he drank: therefore he requested of the prince of the eunuchs that he might not defile himself.   *Daniel 1:8*

Every man according as he purposeth in his heart, so let him give; not grudgingly, or of necessity: for God loveth a cheerful giver.   *2 Corinthians 9:7*

> **CHAMPIONS MAKE DECISIONS THAT CREATE THE FUTURE THEY DESIRE WHILE LOSERS MAKE DECISIONS THAT CREATE THE PRESENT THEY DESIRE.**
> *-MIKE MURDOCK*

DEPRESSION

But Thou, O Lord, art a shield for me; my glory, and the lifter up of mine head. I cried unto the Lord with my voice, and He heard me out of His holy hill. I laid me down and slept; I awaked; for the Lord sustained me. *Psalm 3:3-5*

Weeping may endure for a night, but joy cometh in the morning. *Psalm 30:5*

Our soul waiteth for the Lord: He is our help and our shield. *Psalm 33:20*

Why art thou cast down, O my soul? and why art thou disquieted within me? hope thou in God: for I shall yet praise Him, Who is the health of my countenance, and my God. *Psalm 42:11*

The Lord shall preserve thy going out and thy coming in from this time forth, and even for evermore. *Psalm 121:8*

He healeth the broken in heart, and bindeth up their wounds. *Psalm 147:3*

**STRUGGLE IS THE PROOF
YOU HAVE NOT YET BEEN CONQUERED.
WARFARE ALWAYS SURROUNDS
THE BIRTH OF A MIRACLE.**
-MIKE MURDOCK

DESIRE

Delight thyself also in the Lord: and He shall give thee the desires of thine heart.   *Psalm 37:4*

Lord, all my desire is before Thee; and my groaning is not hid from Thee.
Psalm 38:9

There is none upon earth that I desire beside Thee.   *Psalm 73:25*

The desire accomplished is sweet to the soul: *Proverbs 13:19*

And all things, whatsoever ye shall ask in prayer, believing, ye shall receive.
Matthew 21:22

Therefore I say unto you, What things soever ye desire, when ye pray, believe that ye receive them, and ye shall have them.
Mark 11:24

And I say unto you, Ask, and it shall be given you; seek, and ye shall find; knock, and it shall be opened unto you.
Luke 11:9

THE PROOF OF DESIRE IS PURSUIT. YOU WILL NEVER POSSESS WHAT YOU ARE UNWILLING TO PURSUE. DESIRE IS NOT WHAT YOU WANT, IT IS WHAT YOU CANNOT LIVE WITHOUT. WHATEVER YOU ARE SEEKING IS SOMEWHERE SEEKING YOU.
-MIKE MURDOCK

DILIGENCE

He becometh poor that dealeth with a slack hand: but the hand of the diligent maketh rich. He that gathereth in summer is a wise son: but he that sleepeth in harvest is a son that causeth shame.
Proverbs 10:4,5

The hand of the diligent shall bear rule: The substance of a diligent man is precious. *Proverbs 12:24,27*

The soul of the sluggard desireth, and hath nothing: but the soul of the diligent shall be made fat. *Proverbs 13:4*

Seest thou a man diligent in his business? he shall stand before kings; he shall not stand before mean men.
Proverbs 22:29

Whatsoever thy hand findeth to do, do it with thy might; for there is no work, nor device, nor knowledge, nor wisdom, in the grave, whither thou goest.
Ecclesiastes 9:10

I can do all things through Christ which strengtheneth me.
Philippians 4:13

DILIGENCE IS SPEEDY ATTENTION TO AN ASSIGNED TASK. IT IS INSISTENCE UPON COMPLETION.
-MIKE MURDOCK

DISAPPOINTMENT

Have not I commanded thee? Be
strong and of a good courage; be not afraid,
neither be thou dismayed: for the Lord thy
God is with thee whithersoever thou goest.
Joshua 1:9

The Lord is my light and my salvation;
whom shall I fear? the Lord is the strength
of my life; of whom shall I be afraid? When
the wicked, even mine enemies and my
foes, came upon me to eat up my flesh, they
stumbled and fell. Though an host should
encamp against me, my heart shall not
fear: though war should rise against me,
in this will I be confident. *Psalm 27:1-3*

I will lift up mine eyes unto the hills,
from whence cometh my help. My help
cometh from the Lord, which made heaven
and earth. *Psalm 121:1,2*

And we know that all things work
together for good to them that love God, to
them who are the called according to His
purpose. What shall we then say to these
things? If God be for us, who can be against
us? *Romans 8:28,31*

DISAPPOINTMENT IS MERELY
THE SCHOOL OF DISCOVERY.
-MIKE MURDOCK

DISCIPLINE

Teach me to do Thy will; for Thou art my God: Thy spirit is good; lead me into the land of uprightness.   *Psalm 143:10*

He that spareth his rod hateth his son: but he that loveth him chasteneth him betimes.   *Proverbs 13:24*

Chasten thy son while there is hope, and let not thy soul spare for his crying.   *Proverbs 19:18*

Train up a child in the way he should go: and when he is old, he will not depart from it. Foolishness is bound in the heart of a child; but the rod of correction shall drive it far from him.   *Proverbs 22:6,15*

O Lord, correct me, but with judgment; not in thine anger, lest thou bring me to nothing.   *Jeremiah 10:24*

For whom the Lord loveth He chasteneth, and scourgeth every son whom He receiveth. If ye endure chastening, God dealeth with you as with sons; for what son is he whom the father chasteneth not? But if ye be without chastisement, whereof all are partakers, then are ye bastards, and not sons.   *Hebrews 12:6-8*

CHAMPIONS ARE WILLING
TO DO THINGS THEY HATE
TO CREATE SOMETHING THEY LOVE.
-MIKE MURDOCK

DISCRETION

Give therefore Thy servant an understanding heart to judge Thy people, that I may discern between good and bad: for who is able to judge this Thy so great a people? *1 Kings 3:9*

Blessed is the man that walketh not in the counsel of the ungodly, nor standeth in the way of sinners, nor sitteth in the seat of the scornful. But his delight is in the law of the Lord; and in His law doth he meditate day and night. And he shall be like a tree planted by the rivers of water, that bringeth forth his fruit in his season; his leaf also shall not wither; and whatsoever he doeth shall prosper.
Psalm 1:1-3

A good man sheweth favour, and lendeth: he will guide his affairs with discretion. *Psalm 112:5*

I am Thy servant; give me understanding, that I may know Thy testimonies. The entrance of Thy words giveth light; it giveth understanding unto the simple. *Psalm 119:125,130*

Trust in the Lord with all thine heart; and lean not unto thine own understanding. In all thy ways acknowledge Him, and He shall direct thy paths. *Proverbs 3:5,6*

NEVER DISCUSS YOUR PROBLEM WITH SOMEONE WHO CANNOT SOLVE IT. SILENCE CANNOT BE MISQUOTED.
-MIKE MURDOCK

ENTHUSIASM

Let the heavens be glad, and let the earth rejoice: and let men say among the nations, The Lord reigneth.
1 Chronicles 16:31

Thou hast turned for me my mourning into dancing: *Psalm 30:11*

O clap your hands, all ye people; shout unto God with the voice of triumph.
Psalm 47:1

Blessed is the people that know the joyful sound: they shall walk, O Lord, in the light of Thy countenance.
Psalm 89:15

A merry heart maketh a cheerful countenance: *Proverbs 15:13*

For ye shall go out with joy, and be led forth with peace: *Isaiah 55:12*

Speaking to yourselves in psalms and hymns and spiritual songs, singing and making melody in your heart to the Lord;
Ephesians 5:19

ENTHUSIASM IS THE AWARENESS THAT EVERY NEW BEGINNING BEGINS IN DARKNESS.
-MIKE MURDOCK

ETHICS

Thou shalt not bear false witness against thy neighbor.   *Exodus 20:16*

Blessed is the man that walketh not in the counsel of the ungodly, nor standeth in the way of sinners, nor sitteth in the seat of the scornful. But his delight is in the law of the Lord; and in His law doth he meditate day and night.   *Psalm 1:1,2*

Let integrity and uprightness preserve me; for I wait on thee.
Psalm 25:21

Judge me, O Lord; for I have walked in mine integrity: I have trusted also in the Lord; therefore I shall not slide.
Psalm 26:1

The just man walketh in his integrity: his children are blessed after him.
Proverbs 20:7

Recompense to no man evil for evil. Provide things honest in the sight of all men.   *Romans 12:17*

**WHAT YOU ARE
IS REVEALED BY WHAT YOU DO.
WHAT YOU DO REVEALS
WHAT YOU REALLY BELIEVE.**
-MIKE MURDOCK

EXCELLENCE

The righteous also shall hold on his way, and he that hath clean hands shall be stronger and stronger.   *Job 17:9*

The righteous shall flourish like the palm tree: he shall grow like a cedar in Lebanon.   *Psalm 92:12*

A good name is rather to be chosen than great riches, and loving favour rather than silver and gold.   *Proverbs 22:1*

Then the presidents and princes sought to find occasion against Daniel concerning the kingdom; but they could find none occasion nor fault; forasmuch as he was faithful, neither was there any error or fault found in him.   *Daniel 6:4*

Therefore, as ye abound in every thing, in faith, and utterance, and knowledge, and in all diligence, and in your love to us, see that ye abound in this grace also.   *2 Corinthians 8:7*

THE GREATEST QUALITY OF SUCCESS IS THE WILLINGNESS TO BECOME.
-MIKE MURDOCK

EXPECTATION

Why art thou cast down, O my soul? and why art thou disquieted within me? hope thou in God: for I shall yet praise Him, who is the health of my countenance, and my God. *Psalm 42:11*

My soul, wait thou only upon God; for my expectation is from Him. *Psalm 62:5*

For surely there is an end; and thine expectation shall not be cut off.
Proverbs 23:18

Jesus said unto him, If thou canst believe, all things are possible to him that believeth. *Mark 9:23*

For verily I say unto you, That whosoever shall say unto this mountain, Be thou removed, and be thou cast into the sea; and shall not doubt in his heart, but shall believe that those things which he saith shall come to pass; he shall have whatsoever he saith. Therefore I say unto you, What things soever ye desire, when ye pray, believe that ye receive them, and ye shall have them. *Mark 11:23,24*

But without faith it is impossible to please Him; for he that cometh to God must believe that He is, and that He is a rewarder of them that diligently seek Him.
Hebrews 11:6

THE SEASONS OF YOUR LIFE
WILL CHANGE EVERY TIME YOU DECIDE
TO USE YOUR FAITH.
-MIKE MURDOCK

FAITH

And all things, whatsoever ye shall
ask in prayer, believing, ye shall receive.
Matthew 21:22

Jesus said unto him, If thou canst
believe, all things are possible to him that
believeth.   *Mark 9:23*

Therefore I say unto you, What things
soever ye desire, when ye pray, believe that
ye receive them, and ye shall have them.
Mark 11:24

And the Lord said, If ye had faith as a
grain of mustard seed, ye might say unto
this sycamine tree, Be thou plucked up by
the root, and be thou planted in the sea;
and it should obey you.   *Luke 17:6*

He staggered not at the promise of God
through unbelief; but was strong in faith,
giving glory to God; And being fully
persuaded that, what He had promised, He
was able also to perform. *Romans 4:20,21*

Above all, taking the shield of faith,
wherewith ye shall be able to quench all
the fiery darts of the wicked.
Ephesians 6:16

**WHEN YOU WANT SOMETHING
YOU HAVE NEVER HAD,
YOU HAVE GOT TO DO SOMETHING
YOU HAVE NEVER DONE.**
-MIKE MURDOCK

FAMILY

Train up a child in the way he should go: and when he is old, he will not depart from it.   *Proverbs 22:6*

The father of the righteous shall greatly rejoice: and he that begetteth a wise child shall have joy of him.
                                                    Proverbs 23:24

Through wisdom is an house builded; and by understanding it is established:
                                                    Proverbs 24:3

And all thy children shall be taught of the Lord; and great shall be the peace of thy children.   *Isaiah 54:13*

And they said, Believe on the Lord Jesus Christ, and thou shalt be saved, and thy house.   *Acts 16:31*

And, ye fathers, provoke not your children to wrath: but bring them up in the nurture and admonition of the Lord.
                                                    Ephesians 6:4

But if any provide not for his own, and specially for those of his own house, he hath denied the faith, and is worse than an infidel.   *1 Timothy 5:8*

**YOU ARE THE SEED
THAT DECIDES
THE HARVEST AROUND YOU.**
                                -MIKE MURDOCK

FAVOR

A good man sheweth favour, and lendeth: he will guide his affairs with discretion. *Psalm 112:5*

He that diligently seeketh good procureth favour: but he that seeketh mischief, it shall come unto him.
Proverbs 11:27

A good man obtaineth favour of the Lord: but a man of wicked devices will He condemn. *Proverbs 12:2*

Good understanding giveth favour: but the way of transgressors is hard. Every prudent man dealeth with knowledge: but a fool layeth open his folly.
Proverbs 13:15,16

Favour is deceitful, and beauty is vain: but a woman that feareth the Lord, she shall be praised. *Proverbs 31:30*

And Jesus increased in wisdom and stature, and in favour with God and man.
Luke 2:52

CURRENTS OF FAVOR BEGIN TO FLOW THE MOMENT YOU SOLVE A PROBLEM FOR SOMEONE.
-MIKE MURDOCK

FEAR

Be strong and of a good courage, fear not, nor be afraid of them: for the Lord thy God, He it is that doth go with thee; He will not fail thee, nor forsake thee.
Deuteronomy 31:6

Behold, God is my salvation; I will trust, and not be afraid: for the Lord Jehovah is my strength and my song; He also is become my salvation. *Isaiah 12:2*

Fear thou not; for I am with thee: be not dismayed; for I am thy God: I will strengthen thee; yea, I will help thee; yea, I will uphold thee with the right hand of My righteousness. *Isaiah 41:10*

For ye have not received the spirit of bondage again to fear; but ye have received the Spirit of adoption, whereby we cry, Abba, Father. *Romans 8:15*

For God hath not given us the spirit of fear; but of power, and of love, and of a sound mind. *2 Timothy 1:7*

> **EXAMINE WELL
> WHAT YOU ARE RUNNING FROM.
> YOU ARE NOT PREY.
> YOUR FUTURE IS
> WHIMPERING AT YOUR FEET
> BEGGING FOR INSTRUCTIONS.**
> *-MIKE MURDOCK*

FOCUS

But if from thence thou shalt seek the Lord thy God, thou shalt find Him, if thou seek Him with all thy heart and with all thy soul.
Deuteronomy 4:29

Ye shall observe to do therefore as the Lord your God hath commanded you: ye shall not turn aside to the right hand or to the left.
Deuteronomy 5:32

Only be thou strong and very courageous, that thou mayest observe to do according to all the law, which Moses My servant commanded thee: turn not from it to the right hand or to the left, that thou mayest prosper whithersoever thou goest.
Joshua 1:7

My heart is fixed, O God, my heart is fixed: I will sing and give praise.
Psalm 57:7

And Jesus said unto him, No man, having put his hand to the plough, and looking back, is fit for the kingdom of God.
Luke 9:62

I press toward the mark for the prize of the high calling of God in Christ Jesus.
Philippians 3:14

> **THE ONLY REASON MEN FAIL IS BROKEN FOCUS. YOU WILL ONLY HAVE SIGNIFICANT SUCCESS WITH SOMETHING THAT IS AN OBSESSION.**
> *-MIKE MURDOCK*

FORGIVENESS

The discretion of a man deferreth his anger; and it is his glory to pass over a transgression.   *Proverbs 19:11*

If thine enemy be hungry, give him bread to eat; and if he be thirsty, give him water to drink: *Proverbs 25:21*

Blessed are the merciful: for they shall obtain mercy.   *Matthew 5:7*

But I say unto you, That ye resist not evil: but whosoever shall smite thee on thy right cheek, turn to him the other also.
        Matthew 5:39

But if ye forgive not men their trespasses, neither will your Father forgive your trespasses.   *Matthew 6:15*

And be ye kind one to another, tenderhearted, forgiving one another, even as God for Christ's sake hath forgiven you.
        Ephesians 4:32

Forbearing one another, and forgiving one another,   *Colossians 3:13*

MERCY IS LIKE MONEY,
YOUR DEPOSITS
DETERMINE YOUR WITHDRAWALS.
-MIKE MURDOCK

Friendship

Behold, how good and how pleasant it is for brethren to dwell together in unity!
Psalm 133:1

A friend loveth at all times, and a brother is born for adversity.
Proverbs 17:17

A man that hath friends must shew himself friendly: and there is a friend that sticketh closer than a brother.
Proverbs 18:24

Make no friendship with an angry man;
Proverbs 22:24

Faithful are the wounds of a friend; but the kisses of an enemy are deceitful. Ointment and perfume rejoice the heart: so doth the sweetness of a man's friend by hearty counsel. Thine own friend, and thy father's friend, forsake not; neither go into thy brother's house in the day of thy calamity: for better is a neighbour that is near than a brother far off.
Proverbs 27:6,9,10

Greater love hath no man than this, that a man lay down his life for his friends. Ye are My friends, if ye do whatsoever I command you.
John 15:13,14

> **WHEN GOD WANTS TO BLESS YOU,
> HE PUTS A PERSON IN YOUR LIFE.**
> *-MIKE MURDOCK*

GOAL-SETTING

In all thy ways acknowledge Him, and He shall direct thy paths.   *Proverbs 3:6*

Go to the ant, thou sluggard; consider her ways, and be wise: Which having no guide, overseer, or ruler, Provideth her meat in the summer, and gathereth her food in the harvest.   *Proverbs 6:6-8*

The preparations of the heart in man, and the answer of the tongue, is from the Lord. A man's heart deviseth his way: but the Lord directeth his steps.
Proverbs 16:1,9

For which of you, intending to build a tower, sitteth not down first, and counteth the cost, whether he have sufficient to finish it? Lest haply, after he hath laid the foundation, and is not able to finish it, all that behold it begin to mock him, Saying, This man began to build, and was not able to finish. Or what king, going to make war against another king, sitteth not down first, and consulteth whether he be able with ten thousand to meet him that cometh against him with twenty thousand? Or else, while the other is yet a great way off, he sendeth an ambassage, and desireth conditions of peace.   *Luke 14:28-32*

> **YOU WILL NEVER LEAVE WHERE YOU ARE UNTIL YOU DECIDE WHERE YOU WOULD RATHER BE.**
> *-MIKE MURDOCK*

GOD

In the beginning God created the heaven and the earth. *Genesis 1:1*

The fool hath said in his heart, There is no God. Corrupt are they, and have done abominable iniquity: there is none that doeth good. *Psalm 53:1*

In the beginning was the Word, and the Word was with God, and the Word was God. The same was in the beginning with God. *John 1:1,2*

For it is written, As I live, saith the Lord, every knee shall bow to Me, and every tongue shall confess to God. So then every one of us shall give account of himself to God. *Romans 14:11,12*

For by Him were all things created, that are in heaven, and that are in earth, visible and invisible, whether they be thrones, or dominions, or principalities, or powers: all things were created by Him, and for Him: And He is before all things, and by Him all things consist. *Colossians 1:16,17*

And a voice came out of the throne, saying, Praise our God, all ye His servants, and ye that fear Him, both small and great. *Revelation 19:5*

THE EVIDENCE OF GOD'S PRESENCE FAR OUTWEIGHS THE PROOF OF HIS ABSENCE.
-MIKE MURDOCK

GOSSIP

Whoso privily slandereth his neighbour, him will I cut off: him that hath an high look and a proud heart will not I suffer. *Psalm 101:5*

Set a watch, O Lord, before my mouth; keep the door of my lips. *Psalm 141:3*

For by thy words thou shalt be justified, and by thy words thou shalt be condemned. *Matthew 12:37*

Let no corrupt communication proceed out of your mouth, but that which is good to the use of edifying, that it may minister grace unto the hearers.
Ephesians 4:29

And withal they learn to be idle, wandering about from house to house; and not only idle, but tattlers also and busybodies, speaking things which they ought not. *1 Timothy 5:13*

Wherefore, my beloved brethren, let every man be swift to hear, slow to speak, slow to wrath: *James 1:19*

But let none of you suffer as a murderer, or as a thief, or as an evildoer, or as a busybody in other men's matters.
1 Peter 4:15

FALSE ACCUSATION IS THE LAST STAGE BEFORE SUPERNATURAL PROMOTION.
-MIKE MURDOCK

GRATITUDE

Enter into His gates with thanksgiving, and into His courts with praise: be thankful unto Him, and bless His name. *Psalm 100:4*

And He took the cup, and gave thanks, and said, Take this, and divide it among yourselves: And He took bread, and gave thanks, and brake it, and gave unto them, saying, This is My body which is given for you: this do in remembrance of Me.
Luke 22:17,19

Blessed be the God and Father of our Lord Jesus Christ, who hath blessed us with all spiritual blessings in heavenly places in Christ: *Ephesians 1:3*

Giving thanks always for all things unto God and the Father in the name of our Lord Jesus Christ; *Ephesians 5:20*

Be careful for nothing; but in every thing by prayer and supplication with thanksgiving let your requests be made known unto God. *Philippians 4:6*

Blessing, and glory, and wisdom, and thanksgiving, and honour, and power, and might, be unto our God for ever and ever. Amen. *Revelation 7:12*

GRATITUDE IS SIMPLY AWARENESS OF THE GIVERS IN YOUR LIFE. YOU CANNOT NAME ONE THING THAT WAS NOT GIVEN TO YOU.
-MIKE MURDOCK

GREED

There is that scattereth, and yet increaseth; and there is that withholdeth more than is meet, but it tendeth to poverty. The liberal soul shall be made fat: and he that watereth shall be watered also himself. *Proverbs 11:24,25*

He that despiseth his neighbour sinneth: but he that hath mercy on the poor, happy is he. *Proverbs 14:21*

He that is greedy of gain troubleth his own house; *Proverbs 15:27*

Labour not to be rich: cease from thine own wisdom. Wilt thou set thine eyes upon that which is not? for riches certainly make themselves wings; they fly away as an eagle toward heaven. *Proverbs 23:4,5*

And He said unto them, Take heed, and beware of covetousness: for a man's life consisteth not in the abundance of the things which he possesseth. For where your treasure is, there will your heart be also. *Luke 12:15,34*

Be content with such things as ye have: for He hath said, I will never leave thee, nor forsake thee. *Hebrews 13:5*

GIVING IS THE ONLY PROOF THAT YOU HAVE OVERCOME GREED.
-MIKE MURDOCK

HABITS

So will I sing praise unto Thy name for ever, that I may daily perform my vows.
Psalm 61:8

My son, keep My words, and lay up My commandments with thee.
Proverbs 7:1

Know ye not, that to whom ye yield yourselves servants to obey, his servants ye are to whom ye obey; whether of sin unto death, or of obedience unto righteousness?
Romans 6:16

This I say then, Walk in the Spirit, and ye shall not fulfil the lust of the flesh.
Galatians 5:16

I can do all things through Christ which strengtheneth me. *Philippians 4:13*

Howbeit for this cause I obtained mercy, that in me first Jesus Christ might shew forth all longsuffering, for a pattern to them which should hereafter believe on Him to life everlasting.   *1 Timothy 1:16*

In all things shewing thyself a pattern of good works: in doctrine shewing uncorruptness, gravity, sincerity,
Titus 2:7

MEN DO NOT DECIDE THEIR FUTURE. THEY DECIDE THEIR HABITS AND THEIR HABITS DECIDE THEIR FUTURE. THE SECRET OF YOUR FUTURE IS HIDDEN IN YOUR DAILY ROUTINE.
-MIKE MURDOCK

HAPPINESS

Behold, happy is the man whom God correcteth: therefore despise not thou the chastening of the Almighty: *Job 5:17*

Thou hast put gladness in my heart, more than in the time that their corn and their wine increased.   *Psalm 4:7*

Happy is that people, that is in such a case: yea, happy is that people, whose God is the Lord.   *Psalm 144:15*

Happy is the man that findeth wisdom, and the man that getteth understanding.   *Proverbs 3:13*

He that despiseth his neighbour sinneth: but he that hath mercy on the poor, happy is he.   *Proverbs 14:21*

He that handleth a matter wisely shall find good: and whoso trusteth in the Lord, happy is he.   *Proverbs 16:20*

He that keepeth the law, happy is he.   *Proverbs 29:18*

**HAPPY IS THE MAN
THAT FINDETH WISDOM.
THAT IS HOW YOU KNOW WHO HAS IT.**
-MIKE MURDOCK

HEALTH

I will put none of these diseases upon thee, which have I brought upon the Egyptians: for I am the Lord that healeth thee. *Exodus 15:26*

He healeth the broken in heart, and bindeth up their wounds. *Psalm 147:3*

Be not wise in thine own eyes: fear the Lord, and depart from evil. It shall be health to thy navel, and marrow to thy bones. *Proverbs 3:7,8*

My son, attend to My words; incline thine ear unto My sayings. Let them not depart from thine eyes; keep them in the midst of thine heart. For they are life unto those that find them, and health to all their flesh. *Proverbs 4:20-22*

Pleasant words are as an honeycomb, sweet to the soul, and health to the bones. *Proverbs 16:24*

A merry heart doeth good like a medicine: but a broken spirit drieth the bones. *Proverbs 17:22*

For I will restore health unto thee, and I will heal thee of thy wounds, saith the Lord; *Jeremiah 30:17*

Beloved, I wish above all things that thou mayest prosper and be in health, even as thy soul prospereth. *3 John 1:2*

**LONGEVITY
IS THE PRODUCT OF WISDOM.**
-MIKE MURDOCK

HUMILITY

By humility and the fear of the Lord are riches, and honour, and life.

Proverbs 22:4

Whosoever therefore shall humble himself as this little child, the same is greatest in the kingdom of heaven.

Matthew 18:4

And being found in fashion as a man, He humbled Himself, and became obedient unto death, even the death of the cross.

Philippians 2:8

Put on therefore, as the elect of God, holy and beloved, bowels of mercies, kindness, humbleness of mind, meekness, longsuffering;

Colossians 3:12

But He giveth more grace. Wherefore He saith, God resisteth the proud, but giveth grace unto the humble. Humble yourselves in the sight of the Lord, and He shall lift you up.

James 4:6,10

Humble yourselves therefore under the mighty hand of God, that He may exalt you in due time:

1 Peter 5:6

THOSE IN HIGH PLACES CAN BE BROUGHT DOWN. THOSE IN LOW PLACES CAN BE CALLED UP. HUMILITY IS THE AWARENESS OF IT.

-MIKE MURDOCK

IGNORANCE

Give therefore Thy servant an understanding heart to judge Thy people, that I may discern between good and bad: for who is able to judge this Thy so great a people?   *1 Kings 3:9*

The fear of the Lord is the beginning of wisdom: a good understanding have all they that do His commandments: His praise endureth for ever.   *Psalm 111:10*

For the Lord giveth wisdom: out of His mouth cometh knowledge and understanding. He layeth up sound wisdom for the righteous: He is a buckler to them that walk uprightly.
                    Proverbs 2:6,7

My people are destroyed for lack of knowledge: because thou hast rejected knowledge, I will also reject thee, that thou shalt be no priest to Me: seeing thou hast forgotten the law of thy God, I will also forget thy children.   *Hosea 4:6*

For this cause we also, since the day we heard it, do not cease to pray for you, and to desire that ye might be filled with the knowledge of His will in all wisdom and spiritual understanding; That ye might walk worthy of the Lord unto all pleasing, being fruitful in every good work, and increasing in the knowledge of God;
                    Colossians 1:9,10

> **YOU WILL NEVER CHANGE WHAT YOU BELIEVE UNTIL YOUR BELIEF SYSTEM CANNOT PRODUCE SOMETHING YOU WANT.**
> *-MIKE MURDOCK*

INFORMATION

The entrance of Thy words giveth light; it giveth understanding unto the simple.   *Psalm 119:130*

Whoso loveth instruction loveth knowledge: but he that hateth reproof is brutish.   *Proverbs 12:1*

For God giveth to a man that is good in His sight wisdom, and knowledge, and joy: *Ecclesiastes 2:26*

My people are destroyed for lack of knowledge: because thou hast rejected knowledge, I will also reject thee, that thou shalt be no priest to Me: seeing thou hast forgotten the law of thy God, I will also forget thy children.   *Hosea 4:6*

For this cause we also, since the day we heard it, do not cease to pray for you, and to desire that ye might be filled with the knowledge of His will in all wisdom and spiritual understanding; That ye might walk worthy of the Lord unto all pleasing, being fruitful in every good work, and increasing in the knowledge of God;
                    Colossians 1:9,10

> **THE DIFFERENCE IN PEOPLE IS BETWEEN THEIR EARS. THE DIFFERENCE BETWEEN YOUR PRESENT AND YOUR FUTURE IS INFORMATION.**
> *-MIKE MURDOCK*

INTEGRITY

Let me be weighed in an even balance, that God may know mine integrity.
Job 31:6

Blessed is the man that walketh not in the counsel of the ungodly, nor standeth in the way of sinners, nor sitteth in the seat of the scornful.   *Psalm 1:1*

The fear of the Lord is the beginning of wisdom: a good understanding have all they that do His commandments: His praise endureth for ever.   *Psalm 111:10*

A good man sheweth favour, and lendeth: he will guide his affairs with discretion.   *Psalm 112:5*

The just man walketh in his integrity: his children are blessed after him.
Proverbs 20:7

But if ye have bitter envying and strife in your hearts, glory not, and lie not against the truth.   *James 3:14*

NEVER REWRITE YOUR THEOLOGY
TO ACCOMMODATE A DESIRE.
-MIKE MURDOCK

JESUS

And she shall bring forth a son, and thou shalt call His name Jesus: for He shall save His people from their sins.
Matthew 1:21

For unto you is born this day in the city of David a Saviour, which is Christ the Lord. *Luke 2:11*

Then spake Jesus again unto them, saying, I am the light of the world: he that followeth Me shall not walk in darkness, but shall have the light of life. *John 8:12*

I am the good shepherd: the good shepherd giveth His life for the sheep.
John 10:11

Jesus said unto her, I am the resurrection, and the life: he that believeth in Me, though he were dead, yet shall he live: *John 11:25*

Jesus saith unto him, I am the way, the truth, and the life: no man cometh unto the Father, but by Me. *John 14:6*

For there is one God, and one mediator between God and men, the man Christ Jesus; *1 Timothy 2:5*

> HIS MIND IS KEENER THAN YOURS;
> HIS MEMORY IS LONGER THAN YOURS;
> HIS SHOULDERS ARE BIGGER
> THAN YOURS.
> -MIKE MURDOCK

LEADERSHIP

The steps of a good man are ordered by the Lord: and He delighteth in his way.
Psalm 37:23

For the Lord God is a sun and shield: the Lord will give grace and glory: no good thing will He withhold from them that walk uprightly.
Psalm 84:11

For with what judgment ye judge, ye shall be judged: and with what measure ye mete, it shall be measured to you again.
Matthew 7:2

For as many as are led by the Spirit of God, they are the sons of God.
Romans 8:14

And the things that thou hast heard of me among many witnesses, the same commit thou to faithful men, who shall be able to teach others also.   *2 Timothy 2:2*

Let the elders that rule well be counted worthy of double honour, especially they who labour in the word and doctrine. For the scripture saith, Thou shalt not muzzle the ox that treadeth out the corn. And, The labourer is worthy of his reward. Against an elder receive not an accusation, but before two or three witnesses. Them that sin rebuke before all, that others also may fear.
1 Timothy 5:17-20

THE ABILITY TO FOLLOW IS THE FIRST QUALIFICATION FOR LEADERSHIP.
-MIKE MURDOCK

LONELINESS

And, behold, I am with thee, and will keep thee in all places whither thou goest, and will bring thee again into this land; for I will not leave thee, until I have done that which I have spoken to thee of.
Genesis 28:15

And the Lord, He it is that doth go before thee; He will be with thee, He will not fail thee, neither forsake thee: fear not, neither be dismayed.   *Deuteronomy 31:8*

Yea, though I walk through the valley of the shadow of death, I will fear no evil: for Thou art with me; Thy rod and Thy staff they comfort me.   *Psalm 23:4*

When my father and my mother forsake me, then the Lord will take me up.
Psalm 27:10

I will not leave you comfortless: I will come to you.   *John 14:18*

I will never leave thee, nor forsake thee.   *Hebrews 13:5*

Casting all your care upon Him; for He careth for you.   *1 Peter 5:7*

LONELINESS IS NOT THE ABSENCE OF AFFECTION, BUT THE ABSENCE OF DIRECTION.
-MIKE MURDOCK

LOVE

Many waters cannot quench love, neither can the floods drown it: if a man would give all the substance of his house for love, it would utterly be contemned.
Song of Solomon 8:7

A new commandment I give unto you, That ye love one another; as I have loved you, that ye also love one another. By this shall all men know that ye are My disciples, if ye have love one to another.
John 13:34,35

For the Father Himself loveth you, because ye have loved Me, and have believed that I came out from God.
John 16:27

For this is the message that ye heard from the beginning, that we should love one another.
1 John 3:11

Beloved, let us love one another: for love is of God; and every one that loveth is born of God, and knoweth God. Herein is love, not that we loved God, but that He loved us, and sent His Son to be the propitiation for our sins.
1 John 4:7,10

> **WHAT YOU RESPECT
> YOU WILL ATTRACT,
> WHAT YOU DO NOT RESPECT
> WILL MOVE AWAY FROM YOU.**
> *-MIKE MURDOCK*

LOYALTY

Be strong and of a good courage, fear not, nor be afraid of them: for the Lord thy God, He it is that doth go with thee; He will not fail thee, nor forsake thee.
Deuteronomy 31:6

A good man sheweth favour, and lendeth: he will guide his affairs with discretion.   *Psalm 112:5*

Blessed are they that keep His testimonies, and that seek Him with the whole heart. Thou hast commanded us to keep Thy precepts diligently.
Psalm 119:2,4

Discretion shall preserve thee, understanding shall keep thee:
Proverbs 2:11

A man that hath friends must shew himself friendly: and there is a friend that sticketh closer than a brother.
Proverbs 18:24

Faithful are the wounds of a friend; but the kisses of an enemy are deceitful.
Proverbs 27:6

Recompense to no man evil for evil. Provide things honest in the sight of all men.   *Romans 12:17*

GIVE ANOTHER WHAT HE CANNOT
FIND ANYWHERE ELSE AND
HE WILL KEEP RETURNING.
-MIKE MURDOCK

LYING

I have hated them that regard lying vanities: but I trust in the Lord.
Psalm 31:6

The lip of truth shall be established for ever: but a lying tongue is but for a moment.
Proverbs 12:19

Blessed are ye, when men shall revile you, and persecute you, and shall say all manner of evil against you falsely, for My sake.
Matthew 5:11

Wherefore putting away lying, speak every man truth with his neighbour: for we are members one of another.
Ephesians 4:25

For we know Him that hath said, Vengeance belongeth unto Me, I will recompense, saith the Lord. And again, The Lord shall judge His people.
Hebrews 10:30

But the fearful, and unbelieving, and the abominable, and murderers, and whoremongers, and sorcerers, and idolaters, and all liars, shall have their part in the lake which burneth with fire and brimstone: which is the second death.
Revelation 21:8

> THOSE WHO WILL LIE FOR YOU
> WILL EVENTUALLY LIE ABOUT YOU.
> THOSE WHO SIN WITH YOU
> WILL EVENTUALLY SIN AGAINST YOU.
> *-MIKE MURDOCK*

TOPIC 53

MENTORSHIP

And Joshua the son of Nun was full of the spirit of wisdom; for Moses had laid his hands upon him: and the children of Israel hearkened unto him, and did as the Lord commanded Moses.

Deuteronomy 34:9

And He gave some, apostles; and some, prophets; and some, evangelists; and some, pastors and teachers; For the perfecting of the saints, for the work of the ministry, for the edifying of the body of Christ: *Ephesians 4:11,12*

When I call to remembrance the unfeigned faith that is in thee, which dwelt first in thy grandmother Lois, and thy mother Eunice; and I am persuaded that in thee also. Wherefore I put thee in remembrance that thou stir up the gift of God, which is in thee by the putting on of my hands. *2 Timothy 1:5,6*

Study to shew thyself approved unto God, a workman that needeth not to be ashamed, rightly dividing the word of truth. *2 Timothy 2:15*

> SOMEONE HAS HEARD WHAT YOU HAVE NOT; SOMEONE HAS SEEN WHAT YOU HAVE NOT; SOMEONE KNOWS WHAT YOU DO NOT. YOUR SUCCESS DEPENDS ON YOUR WILLINGNESS TO BE MENTORED BY THEM.
> -MIKE MURDOCK

MIRACLES

Ah Lord God! behold, Thou hast made the heaven and the earth by Thy great power and stretched out arm, and there is nothing too hard for Thee: *Jeremiah 32:17*

Ask, and it shall be given you; seek, and ye shall find; knock, and it shall be opened unto you: *Matthew 7:7*

For verily I say unto you, That whosoever shall say unto this mountain, Be thou removed, and be thou cast into the sea; and shall not doubt in his heart, but shall believe that those things which he saith shall come to pass; he shall have whatsoever he saith. Therefore I say unto you, What things soever ye desire, when ye pray, believe that ye receive them, and ye shall have them. *Mark 11:23,24*

And these signs shall follow them that believe; In My name shall they cast out devils; they shall speak with new tongues; They shall take up serpents; and if they drink any deadly thing, it shall not hurt them; they shall lay hands on the sick, and they shall recover. *Mark 16:17,18*

How God anointed Jesus of Nazareth with the Holy Ghost and with power: Who went about doing good, and healing all that were oppressed of the devil; for God was with Him. *Acts 10:38*

> YOU ARE NEVER AS FAR FROM
> A MIRACLE AS IT FIRST APPEARS.
> *-MIKE MURDOCK*

MOTIVATION

Be strong and of a good courage, fear not, nor be afraid of them: for the Lord thy God, He it is that doth go with thee; He will not fail thee, nor forsake thee.
Deuteronomy 31:6

Have not I commanded thee? Be strong and of a good courage; be not afraid, neither be thou dismayed: for the Lord thy God is with thee whithersoever thou goest.
Joshua 1:9

And he answered, Fear not: for they that be with us are more than they that be with them. *2 Kings 6:16*

Through Thee will we push down our enemies: through Thy name will we tread them under that rise up against us.
Psalm 44:5

Therefore I will look unto the Lord; I will wait for the God of my salvation: my God will hear me. When I sit in darkness, the Lord shall be a light unto me.
Micah 7:7,8

I can do all things through Christ which strengtheneth me. *Philippians 4:13*

DISCONTENTMENT IS THE CATALYST FOR CHANGE. INTOLERANCE OF THE PRESENT CREATES A FUTURE.
-MIKE MURDOCK

OBEDIENCE

Now therefore, if ye will obey My voice indeed, and keep My covenant, then ye shall be a peculiar treasure unto Me above all people: for all the earth is Mine:
Exodus 19:5

But if thou shalt indeed obey His voice, and do all that I speak; then I will be an enemy unto thine enemies, and an adversary unto thine adversaries. For Mine Angel shall go before thee,
Exodus 23:22,23

If ye be willing and obedient, ye shall eat the good of the land: *Isaiah 1:19*

Whether it be good, or whether it be evil, we will obey the voice of the Lord our God, *Jeremiah 42:6*

For as by one man's disobedience many were made sinners, so by the obedience of one shall many be made righteous. *Romans 5:19*

Casting down imaginations, and every high thing that exalteth itself against the knowledge of God, and bringing into captivity every thought to the obedience of Christ; *2 Corinthians 10:5*

Children, obey your parents in the Lord: for this is right. *Ephesians 6:1*

> **GOD WILL NEVER ADVANCE YOU BEYOND YOUR LAST ACT OF DISOBEDIENCE.**
> *-MIKE MURDOCK*

OPPOSITION

Rest in the Lord, and wait patiently for Him: fret not thyself because of him who prospereth in his way, because of the man who bringeth wicked devices to pass.
Psalm 37:7

In my distress I cried unto the Lord, and He heard me. Deliver my soul, O Lord, from lying lips, and from a deceitful tongue.
Psalm 120:1,2

No weapon that is formed against thee shall prosper; and every tongue that shall rise against thee in judgment thou shalt condemn. This is the heritage of the servants of the Lord, and their righteousness is of Me, saith the Lord.
Isaiah 54:17

When the enemy shall come in like a flood, the Spirit of the Lord shall lift up a standard against him.
Isaiah 59:19

And who is he that will harm you, if ye be followers of that which is good?
1 Peter 3:13

Casting all your care upon Him; for He careth for you.
1 Peter 5:7

OPPOSITION IS REALLY THE PROOF OF PROGRESS. SATAN ALWAYS ATTACKS THOSE NEXT IN LINE FOR A PROMOTION.
-MIKE MURDOCK

OVERCOMING

Be not overcome of evil, but overcome evil with good.   *Romans 12:21*

I write unto you, young men, because ye have overcome the wicked one. I write unto you, little children, because ye have known the Father.   *1 John 2:13*

Ye are of God, little children, and have overcome them: because greater is He that is in you, than he that is in the world.
1 John 4:4

To him that overcometh will I give to eat of the tree of life, which is in the midst of the paradise of God.   *Revelation 2:7*

To him that overcometh will I grant to sit with Me in My throne, even as I also overcame, and am set down with My Father in His throne.   *Revelation 3:21*

He that overcometh shall inherit all things; and I will be his God, and he shall be My son.   *Revelation 21:7*

**WHAT YOU FAIL TO MASTER
IN YOUR LIFE
WILL EVENTUALLY MASTER YOU.**
-MIKE MURDOCK

PAIN

Look upon mine affliction and my pain; and forgive all my sins.
Psalm 25:18

Many are the afflictions of the righteous: but the Lord delivereth him out of them all.
Psalm 34:19

Deliver me from the oppression of man:
Psalm 119:134

He healeth the broken in heart, and bindeth up their wounds.
Psalm 147:3

And one shall say unto Him, What are these wounds in thine hands? Then He shall answer, Those with which I was wounded in the house of My friends.
Zechariah 13:6

And God shall wipe away all tears from their eyes; and there shall be no more death, neither sorrow, nor crying, neither shall there be any more pain: for the former things are passed away.
Revelation 21:4

PAIN IS DISCOMFORT
CREATED BY DISORDER.
IT IS NOT YOUR ENEMY BUT
MERELY THE PROOF THAT ONE EXISTS.
-MIKE MURDOCK

PATIENCE

Rest in the Lord, and wait patiently for Him: fret not thyself because of him who prospereth in his way, because of the man who bringeth wicked devices to pass.
Psalm 37:7

I waited patiently for the Lord; and He inclined unto me, and heard my cry.
Psalm 40:1

And not only so, but we glory in tribulations also: knowing that tribulation worketh patience; And patience, experience; and experience, hope: And hope maketh not ashamed; because the love of God is shed abroad in our hearts by the Holy Ghost which is given unto us.
Romans 5:3-5

Rejoicing in hope; patient in tribulation; continuing instant in prayer;
Romans 12:12

And let us not be weary in well doing: for in due season we shall reap, if we faint not.
Galatians 6:9

Knowing this, that the trying of your faith worketh patience. But let patience have her perfect work, that ye may be perfect and entire, wanting nothing.
James 1:3,4

PATIENCE IS THE WEAPON THAT FORCES DECEPTION TO REVEAL ITSELF.
-MIKE MURDOCK

PEACE

I will both lay me down in peace, and sleep: for Thou, Lord, only makest me dwell in safety.   *Psalm 4:8*

Great peace have they which love Thy law: and nothing shall offend them.
                    Psalm 119:165

Thou wilt keep him in perfect peace, whose mind is stayed on Thee: because he trusteth in Thee. Lord, Thou wilt ordain peace for us: for Thou also hast wrought all our works in us.   *Isaiah 26:3,12*

Peace I leave with you, My peace I give unto you: not as the world giveth, give I unto you. Let not your heart be troubled, neither let it be afraid.   *John 14:27*

For to be carnally minded is death; but to be spiritually minded is life and peace.
                    Romans 8:6

But the fruit of the Spirit is love, joy, peace, longsuffering, gentleness, goodness, faith,   *Galatians 5:22*

And the fruit of righteousness is sown in peace of them that make peace.
                    James 3:18

**PEACE IS NOT THE ABSENCE
OF CONFLICT, IT IS THE ABSENCE
OF INNER CONFLICT.**
                    -MIKE MURDOCK

PEER PRESSURE

If thy brother, the son of thy mother, or thy son, or thy daughter, or the wife of thy bosom, or thy friend, which is as thine own soul, entice thee secretly, saying, Let us go and serve other gods, which thou hast not known, thou, nor thy fathers; Thou shalt not consent unto him, nor hearken unto him; neither shall thine eye pity him, neither shalt thou spare, neither shalt thou conceal him: *Deuteronomy 13:6,8*

My son, if sinners entice thee, consent thou not. If they say, Come with us, let us lay wait for blood, let us lurk privily for the innocent without cause: Let us swallow them up alive as the grave; and whole, as those that go down into the pit: We shall find all precious substance, we shall fill our houses with spoil: Cast in thy lot among us; let us all have one purse: My son, walk not thou in the way with them; refrain thy foot from their path: *Proverbs 1:10-15*

For we have not an high priest which cannot be touched with the feeling of our infirmities; but was in all points tempted like as we are, yet without sin. Let us therefore come boldly unto the throne of grace, that we may obtain mercy, and find grace to help in time of need.
          Hebrews 4:15,16

SATAN'S FAVORITE ENTRY POINT INTO YOUR LIFE IS ALWAYS THROUGH SOMEONE CLOSE TO YOU.
          -MIKE MURDOCK

PERSEVERANCE

But He knoweth the way that I take: when He hath tried me, I shall come forth as gold. My foot hath held His steps, His way have I kept, and not declined.
Job 23:10,11

And ye shall be hated of all men for My name's sake: but he that endureth to the end shall be saved.   *Matthew 10:22*

Then said Jesus to those Jews which believed on Him, If ye continue in My word, then are ye My disciples indeed;
John 8:31

As the Father hath loved Me, so have I loved you: continue ye in My love.
John 15:9

Confirming the souls of the disciples, and exhorting them to continue in the faith, and that we must through much tribulation enter into the kingdom of God.
Acts 14:22

And he that overcometh, and keepeth My works unto the end, to him will I give power over the nations: *Revelation 2:26*

**ALL MEN FALL,
THE GREAT ONES GET BACK UP.**
-MIKE MURDOCK

PLANNING

In all thy ways acknowledge Him, and He shall direct thy paths.   *Proverbs 3:6*

Without counsel purposes are disappointed: but in the multitude of counsellors they are established.
Proverbs 15:22

The preparations of the heart in man, and the answer of the tongue, is from the Lord. A man's heart deviseth his way: but the Lord directeth his steps.
Proverbs 16:1,9

There are many devices in a man's heart; nevertheless the counsel of the Lord, that shall stand.   *Proverbs 19:21*

The thoughts of the diligent tend only to plenteousness; but of every one that is hasty only to want.   *Proverbs 21:5*

But the liberal deviseth liberal things; and by liberal things shall he stand.
Isaiah 32:8

For I know the thoughts that I think toward you, saith the Lord, thoughts of peace, and not of evil, to give you an expected end.   *Jeremiah 29:11*

THE SEASON FOR RESEARCH IS NOT THE SEASON FOR MARKETING.
-MIKE MURDOCK

PRAYER

Seek the Lord and His strength, seek His face continually.   *1 Chronicles 16:11*

If My people, which are called by My name, shall humble themselves, and pray, and seek My face, and turn from their wicked ways; then will I hear from heaven, and will forgive their sin, and will heal their land.   *2 Chronicles 7:14*

Watch and pray, that ye enter not into temptation: the spirit indeed is willing, but the flesh is weak.   *Matthew 26:41*

Continue in prayer, and watch in the same with thanksgiving;   *Colossians 4:2*

Pray without ceasing.
    1 Thessalonians 5:17

The effectual fervent prayer of a righteous man availeth much.
    James 5:16

But ye, beloved, building up yourselves on your most holy faith, praying in the Holy Ghost,   *Jude 1:20*

ONE HOUR IN THE PRESENCE OF GOD WILL REVEAL ANY FLAW IN YOUR MOST CAREFULLY LAID PLANS.
-MIKE MURDOCK

PROBLEM SOLVING

Without counsel purposes are disappointed: but in the multitude of counsellors they are established.
Proverbs 15:22

He that handleth a matter wisely shall find good: and whoso trusteth in the Lord, happy is he. *Proverbs 16:20*

For which of you, intending to build a tower, sitteth not down first, and counteth the cost, whether he have sufficient to finish it? *Luke 14:28*

For we have not an high priest which cannot be touched with the feeling of our infirmities; but was in all points tempted like as we are, yet without sin. Let us therefore come boldly unto the throne of grace, that we may obtain mercy, and find grace to help in time of need.
Hebrews 4:15,16

And if we know that He hear us, whatsoever we ask, we know that we have the petitions that we desired of Him.
1 John 5:15

YOU WILL ONLY BE REMEMBERED IN LIFE BY THE PROBLEMS YOU SOLVE AND THE ONES YOU CREATE. YOU WILL ONLY BE PURSUED FOR THE PROBLEMS YOU SOLVE. THE PROBLEM THAT INFURIATES YOU THE MOST IS THE PROBLEM GOD HAS ASSIGNED YOU TO SOLVE.
-MIKE MURDOCK

PRODUCTIVITY

Except the Lord build the house, they labour in vain that build it: except the Lord keep the city, the watchman waketh but in vain. *Psalm 127:1*

A wise man will hear, and will increase learning; and a man of understanding shall attain unto wise counsels: *Proverbs 1:5*

And other fell on good ground, and did yield fruit that sprang up and increased; and brought forth, some thirty, and some sixty, and some an hundred. *Mark 4:8*

Verily, verily, I say unto you, Except a corn of wheat fall into the ground and die, it abideth alone: but if it die, it bringeth forth much fruit. *John 12:24*

I am the vine, ye are the branches: He that abideth in Me, and I in him, the same bringeth forth much fruit: for without Me ye can do nothing. Herein is My Father glorified, that ye bear much fruit; so shall ye be My disciples. *John 15:5,8*

That ye might walk worthy of the Lord unto all pleasing, being fruitful in every good work, and increasing in the knowledge of God; *Colossians 1:10*

THE QUALITY OF YOUR PREPARATION DETERMINES THE QUALITY OF YOUR PERFORMANCE.
-MIKE MURDOCK

PROMOTION

For I will promote thee unto very great honour, and I will do whatsoever thou sayest unto Me: come therefore, I pray thee, curse Me this people.   *Numbers 22:17*

For promotion cometh neither from the east, nor from the west, nor from the south. But God is the judge: He putteth down one, and setteth up another.
Psalm 75:6,7

The wise shall inherit glory: but shame shall be the promotion of fools.
Proverbs 3:35

Wisdom is the principle thing; therefore get wisdom: and with all thy getting get understanding. Exalt her, and she shall promote thee: she shall bring thee to honour, when thou dost embrace her. She shall give to thine head an ornament of grace: a crown of glory shall she deliver to thee.   *Proverbs 4:7-9*

O Lord, I know that the way of man is not in himself: it is not in man that walketh to direct his steps.   *Jeremiah 10:23*

I press toward the mark for the prize of the high calling of God in Christ Jesus.
Philippians 3:14

SOMEONE IS ALWAYS OBSERVING YOU WHO IS CAPABLE OF GREATLY BLESSING YOU. YOU WILL NEVER BE PROMOTED UNTIL YOU BECOME OVERQUALIFIED FOR YOUR PRESENT POSITION.
-MIKE MURDOCK

PROSPERITY

Ye shall diligently keep the commandments of the Lord your God, and His testimonies, and His statutes, which He hath commanded thee. That thou mayest go in and possess the good land which the Lord sware unto thy fathers,
Deuteronomy 6:17,18

If they obey and serve Him, they shall spend their days in prosperity, and their years in pleasures. *Job 36:11*

Blessed is the man that walketh not in the counsel of the ungodly, nor standeth in the way of sinners, nor sitteth in the seat of the scornful. But his delight is in the law of the Lord; and in His law doth he meditate day and night. And he shall be like a tree planted by the rivers of water, that bringeth forth his fruit in his season; his leaf also shall not wither; and whatsoever he doeth shall prosper.
Psalm 1:1-3

Let the Lord be magnified, which hath pleasure in the prosperity of His servant.
Psalm 35:27

Beloved, I wish above all things that thou mayest prosper and be in health, even as thy soul prospereth. *3 John 1:2*

PROSPERITY IS HAVING ENOUGH OF GOD'S PROVISION TO COMPLETE HIS INSTRUCTIONS FOR YOUR LIFE.
-MIKE MURDOCK

PROTECTION

Yea, though I walk through the valley of the shadow of death, I will fear no evil: for Thou art with me; Thy rod and Thy staff they comfort me. Thou preparest a table before me in the presence of mine enemies: Thou anointest my head with oil; my cup runneth over.   *Psalm 23:4,5*

He that dwelleth in the secret place of the most High shall abide under the shadow of the Almighty. He shall cover thee with His feathers, and under His wings shalt thou trust: His truth shall be thy shield and buckler. Thou shalt not be afraid for the terror by night; nor for the arrow that flieth by day; Nor for the pestilence that walketh in darkness; nor for the destruction that wasteth at noonday. A thousand shall fall at thy side, and ten thousand at thy right hand; but it shall not come nigh thee. There shall no evil befall thee, neither shall any plague come nigh thy dwelling. For He shall give His angels charge over thee, to keep thee in all thy ways.   *Psalm 91:1,4-7,10,11*

And I will rebuke the devourer for your sakes, and He shall not destroy the fruits of your ground; neither shall your vine cast her fruit before the time in the field, saith the Lord of hosts.   *Malachi 3:11*

PROTECTION IS PRODUCED THROUGH PARTNERSHIP.
-MIKE MURDOCK

RACISM

A new commandment I give unto you, That ye love one another; as I have loved you, that ye also love one another.
John 13:34

There is neither Jew nor Greek, there is neither bond nor free, there is neither male nor female: for ye are all one in Christ Jesus.
Galatians 3:28

And walk in love, as Christ also hath loved us, and hath given Himself for us an offering and a sacrifice to God for a sweetsmelling savour.
Ephesians 5:2

But he that doeth wrong shall receive for the wrong which he hath done: and there is no respect of persons.
Colossians 3:25

If ye fulfil the royal law according to the scripture, Thou shalt love thy neighbour as thyself, ye do well: But if ye have respect to persons, ye commit sin, and are convinced of the law as transgressors.
James 2:8,9

> **YOUR SIGNIFICANCE IS NOT IN YOUR SIMILARITY TO ANOTHER BUT IN YOUR POINT OF DIFFERENCE FROM ANOTHER.**
> *-MIKE MURDOCK*

REPUTATION

Blessed is the man that walketh not in the counsel of the ungodly, nor standeth in the way of sinners, nor sitteth in the seat of the scornful. But his delight is in the law of the Lord; and in His law doth he meditate day and night.   *Psalm 1:1,2*

All the paths of the Lord are mercy and truth unto such as keep His covenant and His testimonies. Let integrity and uprightness preserve me; for I wait on thee.
Psalm 25:10,21

But as for me, I will walk in mine integrity: redeem me, and be merciful unto me.   *Psalm 26:11*

He that handleth a matter wisely shall find good: and whoso trusteth in the Lord, happy is he.   *Proverbs 16:20*

But made Himself of no reputation, and took upon Him the form of a servant, and was made in the likeness of men: And being found in fashion as a man, He humbled Himself, and became obedient unto death, even the death of the cross.
Philippians 2:7,8

> **YOU WILL BE REMEMBERED FOR THE PAIN OR THE PLEASURE YOU HAVE CREATED.**
> *-MIKE MURDOCK*

RESPONSIBILITY

Let us hear the conclusion of the whole matter: Fear God, and keep His commandments: for this is the whole duty of man. *Ecclesiastes 12:13*

Ye are the salt of the earth: but if the salt have lost his savour, wherewith shall it be salted? it is thenceforth good for nothing, but to be cast out, and to be trodden under foot of men. Ye are the light of the world. A city that is set on an hill cannot be hid. Neither do men light a candle, and put it under a bushel, but on a candlestick; and it giveth light unto all that are in the house. Let your light so shine before men, that they may see your good works, and glorify your Father which is in heaven. Whosoever therefore shall break one of these least commandments, and shall teach men so, he shall be called the least in the kingdom of heaven: but whosoever shall do and teach them, the same shall be called great in the kingdom of heaven. *Matthew 5:13-16,19*

Then said Jesus unto His disciples, If any man will come after Me, let him deny himself, and take up his cross, and follow Me. For whosoever will save his life shall lose it: and whosoever will lose his life for My sake shall find it. *Matthew 16:24,25*

WHEN YOU DO WHAT YOU CAN, GOD WILL DO WHAT YOU CANNOT.
-MIKE MURDOCK

REST

And on the seventh day God ended His work which He had made; and He rested on the seventh day from all His work which He had made.   *Genesis 2:2*

Therefore my heart is glad, and my glory rejoiceth: my flesh also shall rest in hope.   *Psalm 16:9*

To every thing there is a season, and a time to every purpose under the heaven: A time to love, and a time to hate; a time of war, and a time of peace.
     Ecclesiastes 3:1,8

For with stammering lips and another tongue will he speak to this people. To whom he said, This is the rest wherewith ye may cause the weary to rest; and this is the refreshing: yet they would not hear.
     Isaiah 28:11,12

Come unto Me, all ye that labour and are heavy laden, and I will give you rest.
     Matthew 11:28

Take My yoke upon you, and learn of Me; for I am meek and lowly in heart: and ye shall find rest unto your souls. For My yoke is easy, and My burden is light.
     Matthew 11:29,30

> **WHEN FATIGUE WALKS IN FAITH WALKS OUT. TIRED EYES RARELY SEE A GOOD FUTURE.**
> *-MIKE MURDOCK*

RICHES

But thou shalt remember the Lord thy God: for it is He that giveth thee power to get wealth, that He may establish His covenant which He sware unto thy fathers, as it is this day. *Deuteronomy 8:18*

Praise ye the Lord. Blessed is the man that feareth the Lord, that delighteth greatly in His commandments. His seed shall be mighty upon earth: the generation of the upright shall be blessed. Wealth and riches shall be in his house: and his righteousness endureth for ever.
Psalm 112:1-3

Happy is the man that findeth wisdom, and the man that getteth understanding. Length of days is in her right hand; and in her left hand riches and honour. *Proverbs 3:13,16*

The wealth of the sinner is laid up for the just. *Proverbs 13:22*

Lay not up for yourselves treasures upon earth, where moth and rust doth corrupt, and where thieves break through and steal: But lay up for yourselves treasures in heaven, where neither moth nor rust doth corrupt, and where thieves do not break through nor steal:
Matthew 6:19,20

SOME STUDY THE EXIT OF EVERY PENNY, OTHERS STUDY THE ENTRY OF EVERY DOLLAR. THE WISE DO BOTH.
-MIKE MURDOCK

SALVATION

All we like sheep have gone astray; we have turned every one to his own way; and the Lord hath laid on Him the iniquity of us all.   *Isaiah 53:6*

But as many as received Him, to them gave He power to become the sons of God, even to them that believe on His name:
                                    John 1:12

Him that cometh to Me I will in no wise cast out.   *John 6:37*

And they said, Believe on the Lord Jesus Christ, and thou shalt be saved, and thy house.   *Acts 16:31*

For all have sinned, and come short of the glory of God;   *Romans 3:23*

That if thou shalt confess with thy mouth the Lord Jesus, and shalt believe in thine heart that God hath raised Him from the dead, thou shalt be saved. For with the heart man believeth unto righteousness; and with the mouth confession is made unto salvation.
                                    Romans 10:9,10

GOD NEVER CONSULTS YOUR PAST TO DETERMINE YOUR FUTURE.
-MIKE MURDOCK

SCHEDULE

Commit thy way unto the Lord; trust also in Him; and He shall bring it to pass.
Psalm 37:5

And let the beauty of the Lord our God be upon us: and establish thou the work of our hands upon us; yea, the work of our hands establish thou it. *Psalm 90:17*

To every thing there is a season, and a time to every purpose under the heaven: A time to kill, and a time to heal; a time to break down, and a time to build up;
Ecclesiastes 3:1,3

And thine ears shall hear a word behind thee, saying, This is the way, walk ye in it, when ye turn to the right hand, and when ye turn to the left. *Isaiah 30:21*

For the vision is yet for an appointed time, but at the end it shall speak, and not lie: though it tarry, wait for it; because it will surely come, it will not tarry.
Habakkuk 2:3

And let us not be weary in well doing: for in due season we shall reap, if we faint not. *Galatians 6:9*

Redeeming the time, because the days are evil. *Ephesians 5:16*

> **THOSE WHO DO NOT RESPECT YOUR TIME WILL NOT RESPECT YOUR WISDOM EITHER.**
> *-MIKE MURDOCK*

SEED-FAITH

While the earth remaineth, seedtime and harvest, and cold and heat, and summer and winter, and day and night shall not cease. *Genesis 8:22*

Vow, and pay unto the Lord your God: let all that be round about Him bring presents unto Him that ought to be feared. *Psalm 76:11*

Honour the Lord with thy substance, and with the firstfruits of all thine increase: So shall thy barns be filled with plenty, and thy presses shall burst out with new wine. *Proverbs 3:9,10*

Cast thy bread upon the waters: for thou shalt find it after many days. In the morning sow thy seed, and in the evening withhold not thine hand: for thou knowest not whether shall prosper, either this or that, or whether they both shall be alike good. *Ecclesiastes 11:1,6*

Give, and it shall be given unto you; good measure, pressed down, and shaken together, and running over, shall men give into your bosom. For with the same measure that ye mete withal it shall be measured to you again. *Luke 6:38*

But this I say, He which soweth sparingly shall reap also sparingly; and he which soweth bountifully shall reap also bountifully. *2 Corinthians 9:6*

SEED-FAITH IS SOWING WHAT YOU HAVE BEEN GIVEN TO CREATE WHAT YOU HAVE BEEN PROMISED.
-MIKE MURDOCK

SELF-CONFIDENCE

The Lord is my light and my salvation; whom shall I fear? the Lord is the strength of my life; of whom shall I be afraid?
Psalm 27:1

It is better to trust in the Lord than to put confidence in man.   *Psalm 118:8*

For the Lord shall be thy confidence, and shall keep thy foot from being taken.
Proverbs 3:26

Behold, I have graven thee upon the palms of My hands;   *Isaiah 49:16*

Ye have not chosen Me, but I have chosen you,   *John 15:16*

Being confident of this very thing, that He which hath begun a good work in you will perform it until the day of Jesus Christ: *Philippians 1:6*

I can do all things through Christ which strengtheneth me. *Philippians 4:13*

Ye are of God, little children, and have overcome them: because greater is He that is in you, than he that is in the world.
1 John 4:4

SOMEBODY HAS BEEN WAITING FOR YOU A LIFETIME.
-MIKE MURDOCK

SEX

He that covereth his sins shall not prosper: but whoso confesseth and forsaketh them shall have mercy.
Proverbs 28:13

Flee fornication. Every sin that a man doeth is without the body; but he that committeth fornication sinneth against his own body.   *1 Corinthians 6:18*

What? know ye not that your body is the temple of the Holy Ghost which is in you, which ye have of God, and ye are not your own? Therefore glorify God in your body, and in your spirit, which are God's.
1 Corinthians 6:19,20

Nevertheless, to avoid fornication, let every man have his own wife, and let every woman have her own husband.
1 Corinthians 7:2

There hath no temptation taken you but such as is common to man: but God is faithful, Who will not suffer you to be tempted above that ye are able; but will with the temptation also make a way to escape, that ye may be able to bear it.
1 Corinthians 10:13

POWER IS THE ABILITY TO WALK AWAY FROM SOMETHING YOU DESIRE TO PROTECT SOMETHING YOU LOVE.
-MIKE MURDOCK

SIN

Remember not the sins of my youth, nor my transgressions: according to Thy mercy remember Thou me for Thy goodness' sake, O Lord.   *Psalm 25:7*

Hide Thy face from my sins, and blot out all mine iniquities.   *Psalm 51:9*

If I regard iniquity in my heart, the Lord will not hear me: *Psalm 66:18*

Who forgiveth all thine iniquities; Who healeth all thy diseases;
                              Psalm 103:3

With my whole heart have I sought Thee: O let me not wander from Thy commandments. Thy word have I hid in mine heart, that I might not sin against Thee.   *Psalm 119:10,11*

He that covereth his sins shall not prosper: but whoso confesseth and forsaketh them shall have mercy.
                              Proverbs 28:13

For all have sinned, and come short of the glory of God;   *Romans 3:23*

WHAT YOU FAIL TO DESTROY IN YOUR LIFE WILL EVENTUALLY DESTROY YOU.
                              -MIKE MURDOCK

SOUL WINNING

The fruit of the righteous is a tree of life; and he that winneth souls is wise.
Proverbs 11:30

Then saith He unto His disciples, The harvest truly is plenteous, but the labourers are few;
Matthew 9:37

He that is not with Me is against Me; and he that gathereth not with Me scattereth abroad.
Matthew 12:30

And He said unto them, Go ye into all the world, and preach the gospel to every creature. He that believeth and is baptized shall be saved; but he that believeth not shall be damned.
Mark 16:15,16

Jesus answered and said unto him, Verily, verily, I say unto thee, Except a man be born again, he cannot see the kingdom of God.
John 3:3

Say not ye, There are yet four months, and then cometh harvest? behold, I say unto you, Lift up your eyes, and look on the fields; for they are white already to harvest.
John 4:35

THE BROKEN BECOME MASTERS
AT MENDING.
-MIKE MURDOCK

STRESS

The Lord also will be a refuge for the oppressed, a refuge in times of trouble.
Psalm 9:9

What time I am afraid, I will trust in Thee.
Psalm 56:3

My flesh and my heart faileth: but God is the strength of my heart, and my portion for ever.
Psalm 73:26

A thousand shall fall at thy side, and ten thousand at thy right hand; but it shall not come nigh thee. There shall no evil befall thee, neither shall any plague come nigh thy dwelling.
Psalm 91:7,10

It is vain for you to rise up early, to sit up late, to eat the bread of sorrows: for so He giveth His beloved sleep.
Psalm 127:2

Peace I leave with you, My peace I give unto you: not as the world giveth, give I unto you. Let not your heart be troubled, neither let it be afraid.
John 14:27

Casting all your care upon Him; for He careth for you.
1 Peter 5:7

NEVER COMPLAIN ABOUT WHAT YOU PERMIT.
-MIKE MURDOCK

SUCCESS

And he said unto me, The Lord, before Whom I walk, will send His angel with thee, and prosper thy way;   *Genesis 24:40*

Keep therefore the words of this covenant, and do them, that ye may prosper in all that ye do.   *Deuteronomy 29:9*

Only be thou strong and very courageous, that thou mayest observe to do according to all the law, which Moses My servant commanded thee: turn not from it to the right hand or to the left, that thou mayest prosper whithersoever thou goest. This book of the law shall not depart out of thy mouth; but thou shalt meditate therein day and night, that thou mayest observe to do according to all that is written therein: for then thou shalt make thy way prosperous, and then thou shalt have good success.   *Joshua 1:7,8*

Pray for the peace of Jerusalem: they shall prosper that love thee.   *Psalm 122:6*

Honour the Lord with thy substance, and with the firstfruits of all thine increase: So shall thy barns be filled with plenty, and thy presses shall burst out with new wine.   *Proverbs 3:9,10*

YOUR SUCCESS IS DETERMINED BY THE PROBLEMS YOU SOLVE FOR OTHERS.
-MIKE MURDOCK

SUICIDAL THOUGHTS

Thou shalt not kill.   *Exodus 20:13*

The Lord is my light and my salvation; whom shall I fear? the Lord is the strength of my life; of whom shall I be afraid? Though an host should encamp against me, my heart shall not fear: though war should rise against me, in this will I be confident. For in the time of trouble He shall hide me in His pavilion: in the secret of His tabernacle shall He hide me; He shall set me up upon a rock.   *Psalm 27:1,3,5*

Weeping may endure for a night, but joy cometh in the morning.   *Psalm 30:5*

Thy word have I hid in mine heart, that I might not sin against Thee.
Psalm 119:11

I will praise Thee; for I am fearfully and wonderfully made: marvellous are Thy works; and that my soul knoweth right well.   *Psalm 139:14*

Being confident of this very thing, that He which hath begun a good work in you will perform it until the day of Jesus Christ: *Philippians 1:6*

YOUR FOCUS DETERMINES WHAT YOU FEEL. WHEN YOU CHANGE YOUR FOCUS, YOU CHANGE YOUR FEELINGS.
-MIKE MURDOCK

TEAMWORK

Behold, how good and how pleasant it is for brethren to dwell together in unity!
Psalm 133:1

Two are better than one; because they have a good reward for their labour. For if they fall, the one will lift up his fellow: but woe to him that is alone when he falleth; for he hath not another to help him up. And if one prevail against him, two shall withstand him; and a threefold cord is not quickly broken.   *Ecclesiastes 4:9,10,12*

Can two walk together, except they be agreed?   *Amos 3:3*

Again I say unto you, That if two of you shall agree on earth as touching any thing that they shall ask, it shall be done for them of My Father which is in heaven.
Matthew 18:19

And when the day of Pentecost was fully come, they were all with one accord in one place.   *Acts 2:1*

Knowing that whatsoever good thing any man doeth, the same shall he receive of the Lord, whether he be bond or free.
Ephesians 6:8

WHAT YOU MAKE HAPPEN FOR OTHERS,
GOD WILL MAKE HAPPEN FOR YOU.
-MIKE MURDOCK

TEMPTATION

Thy word have I hid in mine heart, that I might not sin against Thee.
Psalm 119:11

When the enemy shall come in like a flood, the Spirit of the Lord shall lift up a standard against him.   *Isaiah 59:19*

There hath no temptation taken you but such as is common to man: but God is faithful, Who will not suffer you to be tempted above that ye are able; but will with the temptation also make a way to escape, that ye may be able to bear it.
1 Corinthians 10:13

Put on the whole armour of God, that ye may be able to stand against the wiles of the devil. Above all, taking the shield of faith, wherewith ye shall be able to quench all the fiery darts of the wicked.
Ephesians 6:11,16

Submit yourselves therefore to God. Resist the devil, and he will flee from you.
James 4:7

The Lord knoweth how to deliver the godly out of temptations,   *2 Peter 2:9*

WHAT YOU ARE WILLING TO WALK AWAY FROM DETERMINES WHAT GOD WILL BRING TO YOU.
-MIKE MURDOCK

TEN COMMANDMENTS

Thou shalt have no other gods before Me. Thou shalt not make unto thee any graven image, or any likeness of any thing that is in heaven above, or that is in the earth beneath, or that is in the water under the earth: Thou shalt not bow down thyself to them, nor serve them: for I the Lord thy God am a jealous God, Thou shalt not take the name of the Lord thy God in vain; for the Lord will not hold him guiltless that taketh His name in vain. Remember the Sabbath day, to keep it holy. Six days shalt thou labour, and do all thy work: But the seventh day is the Sabbath of the Lord thy God: Honour thy father and thy mother: that thy days may be long upon the land which the Lord thy God giveth thee. Thou shalt not kill. Thou shalt not commit adultery. Thou shalt not steal. Thou shalt not bear false witness against thy neighbour. Thou shalt not covet.
Exodus 20:3-5,7-10,12-17

Thou knowest the commandments, Do not commit adultery, Do not kill, Do not steal, Do not bear false witness, Defraud not, Honour thy father and mother. And he answered and said unto Him, Master, all these have I observed from my youth.
Mark 10:19,20

YOUR FUTURE IS DETERMINED BY YOUR ABILITY TO FOLLOW INSTRUCTIONS.
-MIKE MURDOCK

THOUGHTS

Many, O Lord my God, are Thy wonderful works which Thou hast done, and Thy thoughts which are to us-ward: they cannot be reckoned up in order unto Thee: if I would declare and speak of them, they are more than can be numbered.
Psalm 40:5

The thoughts of the righteous are right: but the counsels of the wicked are deceit.   *Proverbs 12:5*

Commit thy works unto the Lord, and thy thoughts shall be established.
Proverbs 16:3

For as he thinketh in his heart, so is he: *Proverbs 23:7*

For I know the thoughts that I think toward you, saith the Lord, thoughts of peace, and not of evil, to give you an expected end.   *Jeremiah 29:11*

Finally, brethren, whatsoever things are true, whatsoever things are honest, whatsoever things are just, whatsoever things are pure, whatsoever things are lovely, whatsoever things are of good report; if there be any virtue, and if there be any praise, think on these things.
Philippians 4:8

LOSERS FOCUS ON WHAT THEY ARE GOING THROUGH WHILE CHAMPIONS FOCUS ON WHAT THEY ARE GOING TO.
-MIKE MURDOCK

TITHING

Thou shalt truly tithe all the increase of thy seed, that the field bringeth forth year by year. *Deuteronomy 14:22*

Honour the Lord with thy substance, and with the firstfruits of all thine increase: So shall thy barns be filled with plenty, and thy presses shall burst out with new wine. *Proverbs 3:9,10*

Bring ye all the tithes into the storehouse, that there may be meat in Mine house, and prove Me now herewith, saith the Lord of hosts, if I will not open you the windows of heaven, and pour you out a blessing, that there shall not be room enough to receive it. And I will rebuke the devourer for your sakes, and he shall not destroy the fruits of your ground; neither shall your vine cast her fruit before the time in the field, saith the Lord of hosts. *Malachi 3:10,11*

Woe unto you, scribes and Pharisees, hypocrites! for ye pay tithe of mint and anise and cummin, and have omitted the weightier matters of the law, judgment, mercy, and faith: these ought ye to have done, and not to leave the other undone. *Matthew 23:23*

WHEN YOU LET GO OF WHAT IS IN YOUR HAND, GOD WILL LET GO OF WHAT IS IN HIS HAND. TITHE IS A MEASURE OF YOUR OBEDIENCE, AN OFFERING IS A MEASURE OF YOUR GENEROSITY.
-MIKE MURDOCK

TRUTH

God is not a man, that He should lie; neither the son of man, that He should repent: hath He said, and shall He not do it? or hath He spoken, and shall He not make it good? *Numbers 23:19*

All the paths of the Lord are mercy and truth unto such as keep His covenant and His testimonies. *Psalm 25:10*

Jesus saith unto him, I am the way, the truth, and the life: no man cometh unto the Father, but by Me. *John 14:6*

Finally, brethren, whatsoever things are true, whatsoever things are honest, whatsoever things are just, whatsoever things are pure, whatsoever things are lovely, whatsoever things are of good report; if there be any virtue, and if there be any praise, think on these things. *Philippians 4:8*

Seeing ye have purified your souls in obeying the truth through the Spirit unto unfeigned love of the brethren, see that ye love one another with a pure heart fervently: *1 Peter 1:22*

TRUTH IS THE MOST POWERFUL THING ON EARTH BECAUSE IT IS THE ONLY THING THAT CANNOT BE CHANGED.
-MIKE MURDOCK

UNEMPLOYMENT

Trust in the Lord, and do good; so shalt thou dwell in the land, and verily thou shalt be fed.   *Psalm 37:3*

Love not sleep, lest thou come to poverty; open thine eyes, and thou shalt be satisfied with bread.   *Proverbs 20:13*

Whatsoever thy hand findeth to do, do it with thy might;   *Ecclesiastes 9:10*

Behold, I will do a new thing; now it shall spring forth; shall ye not know it? I will even make a way in the wilderness, and rivers in the desert.   *Isaiah 43:19*

For verily I say unto you, That whosoever shall say unto this mountain, Be thou removed, and be thou cast into the sea; and shall not doubt in his heart, but shall believe that those things which he saith shall come to pass; he shall have whatsoever he saith.   *Mark 11:23*

For even when we were with you, this we commanded you, that if any would not work, neither should he eat.
2 Thessalonians 3:10

GO WHERE YOU ARE CELEBRATED, NOT WHERE YOU ARE TOLERATED.
-MIKE MURDOCK

VICTORY

Then sang Moses and the children of Israel this song unto the Lord, and spake, saying, I will sing unto the Lord, for He hath triumphed gloriously: the horse and his rider hath He thrown into the sea.
Exodus 15:1

O my God, I trust in Thee: let me not be ashamed, let not mine enemies triumph over me.
Psalm 25:2

For Thou, Lord, hast made me glad through Thy work: I will in the works of Thy hands.
Psalm 92:4

Save us, O Lord our God, and gather us from among the heathen, to give thanks unto Thy holy name, and to triumph in Thy praise.
Psalm 106:47

I can do all things through Christ which strengtheneth me.
Philippians 4:13

And they overcame him by the blood of the Lamb, and by the word of their testimony; and they loved not their lives unto the death.
Revelation 12:11

> YOU WILL NEVER REACH THE PALACE TALKING LIKE A PEASANT.
> -MIKE MURDOCK

VISION

In a dream, in a vision of the night, when deep sleep falleth upon men, in slumberings upon the bed; Then He openeth the ears of men, and sealeth their instruction, That He may withdraw man from his purpose, and hide pride from man.
Job 33:15-17

Where there is no vision, the people perish: but he that keepeth the law, happy is he.   *Proverbs 29:18*

Enlarge the place of thy tent, and let them stretch forth the curtains of thine habitations: spare not, lengthen thy cords, and strengthen thy stakes;   *Isaiah 54:2*

And it shall come to pass afterward, that I will pour out My spirit upon all flesh; and your sons and your daughters shall prophesy, your old men shall dream dreams, your young men shall see visions:
Joel 2:28

Write the vision, and make it plain upon tables, that he may run that readeth it. For the vision is yet for an appointed time, but at the end it shall speak, and not lie; though it tarry, wait for it; because it will surely come, it will not tarry.
Habakkuk 2:2,3

> **STOP LOOKING AT WHERE YOU HAVE BEEN AND START LOOKING AT WHERE YOU CAN BE.**
> *-MIKE MURDOCK*

VOWS

If a man vow a vow unto the Lord, or swear an oath to bind his soul with a bond; he shall not break his word, he shall do according to all that proceedeth out of his mouth. *Numbers 30:2*

When thou shalt vow a vow unto the Lord thy God, thou shalt not slack to pay it: for the Lord thy God will surely require it of thee; and it would be sin in thee. *Deuteronomy 23:21*

Vow, and pay unto the Lord your God: let all that be round about Him bring presents unto Him that ought to be feared. *Psalm 76:11*

He that hath pity upon the poor lendeth unto the Lord; and that which he hath given will He pay him again. *Proverbs 19:17*

Better is it that thou shouldest not vow, than that thou shouldest vow and not pay. *Ecclesiastes 5:5*

And Paul after this tarried there yet a good while, and then took his leave of the brethren, and sailed thence into Syria, and with him Priscilla and Aquila; having shorn his head in Cenchrea: for he had a vow. *Acts 18:18*

> **THE WAVES OF YESTERDAY'S BROKEN VOWS WILL SPLASH ON THE SHORES OF TOMORROW.**
> *-MIKE MURDOCK*

WEALTH

But thou shalt remember the Lord thy God: for it is He that giveth thee power to get wealth, that He may establish His covenant which He sware unto thy fathers, as it is this day.   *Deuteronomy 8:18*

Praise ye the Lord. Blessed is the man that feareth the Lord, that delighteth greatly in His commandments. His seed shall be mighty upon earth: the generation of the upright shall be blessed. Wealth and riches shall be in his house: and his righteousness endureth for ever.   *Psalm 112:1-3*

The wealth of the sinner is laid up for the just.   *Proverbs 13:22*

And He said unto them, Take heed, and beware of covetousness: for a man's life consisteth not in the abundance of the things which he possesseth.   *Luke 12:15*

Charge them that are rich in this world, that they be not highminded, nor trust in uncertain riches, but in the living God, who giveth us richly all things to enjoy; That they do good, that they be rich in good works, ready to distribute, willing to communicate; Laying up in store for themselves a good foundation against the time to come, that they may lay hold on eternal life.   *1 Timothy 6:17-19*

WEALTH IS WHEN YOU HAVE A LOT OF SOMETHING YOU LOVE.
-MIKE MURDOCK

WINNING

Then sang Moses and the children of Israel this song unto the Lord, and spake, saying, I will sing unto the Lord, for He hath triumphed gloriously: the horse and his rider hath he thrown into the sea. *Exodus 15:1*

For Thou, Lord, hast made me glad through Thy work: I will triumph in the works of Thy hands. *Psalm 92:4*

The fruit of the righteous is a tree of life; and he that winneth souls is wise.
Proverbs 11:30

And such as do wickedly against the covenant shall he corrupt by flatteries: but the people that do know their God shall be strong, and do exploits. *Daniel 11:32*

Then he answered and spake unto me, saying, This is the word of the Lord unto Zerubbabel, saying, Not by might, nor by power, but by My spirit, saith the Lord of hosts.
Zechariah 4:6

For I will give you a mouth and wisdom, which all your adversaries shall not be able to gainsay nor resist. *Luke 21:15*

Ye are of God, little children, and have overcome them: because greater is He that is in you, than he that is in the world.
1 John 4:4

> **YOU WILL NEVER OUTGROW WARFARE.**
> **YOU SIMPLY MUST LEARN TO FIGHT.**
> *-MIKE MURDOCK*

Wisdom

Wisdom and knowledge is granted unto thee; and I will give thee riches, and wealth, and honour, such as none of the kings have had that have been before thee, neither shall there any after thee have the like. *2 Chronicles 1:12*

The fear of the Lord is the beginning of wisdom: a good understanding have all they that do His commandments: His praise endureth for ever. *Psalm 111:10*

Happy is the man that findeth wisdom, and the man that getteth understanding. *Proverbs 3:13*

Wisdom is the principle thing; therefore get wisdom: and with all thy getting get understanding. *Proverbs 4:7*

Exalt her, and she shall promote thee: she shall bring thee to honour, when thou dost embrace her. *Proverbs 4:8*

If any of you lack wisdom, let him ask of God, that giveth to all men liberally, and upbraideth not; and it shall be given him. *James 1:5*

> **WISDOM IS THE ONLY REAL NEED YOU WILL EVER HAVE.**
> *-MIKE MURDOCK*

WORK

Six days shalt thou labour, and do all
thy work: *Exodus 20:9*

Six days shall work be done, but on
the seventh day there shall be to you an
holy day, a sabbath of rest to the Lord:
                                  Exodus 35:2

That the Lord thy God may bless thee
in all the work of thine hands.
                              Deuteronomy 24:19

For the people had a mind to work.
                                Nehemiah 4:6

Seest thou a man diligent in his
business? he shall stand before kings; he
shall not stand before mean men.
                               Proverbs 22:29

Be strong, all ye people of the land,
saith the Lord, and work: for I am with
you, saith the Lord of hosts: *Haggai 2:4*

For the workman is worthy of his
meat.   *Matthew 10:10*

Moreover it is required in stewards,
that a man be found faithful.
                             1 Corinthians 4:2

And having food and raiment let us
be therewith content.   *1 Timothy 6:8*

**MONEY IS MERELY A REWARD
FOR SOLVING PROBLEMS.**
                                -MIKE MURDOCK

WORRY

And thou shalt be secure, because there is hope; yea, thou shalt dig about thee, and thou shalt take thy rest in safety.   *Job 11:18*

Fret not thyself because of evil men, neither be thou envious at the wicked;
Proverbs 24:19

In righteousness shalt thou be established: thou shalt be far from oppression; for thou shalt not fear: and from terror; for it shall not come near thee.   *Isaiah 54:14*

Are not two sparrows sold for a farthing? and one of them shall not fall on the ground without your Father. But the very hairs of your head are all numbered. Fear ye not therefore, ye are of more value than many sparrows.
Matthew 10:29-31

Be careful for nothing; but in every thing by prayer and supplication with thanksgiving let your requests be made known unto God. And the peace of God, which passeth all understanding, shall keep your hearts and minds through Christ Jesus. Finally, brethren, whatsoever things are true, whatsoever things are honest, whatsoever things are just, whatsoever things are pure, whatsoever things are lovely, whatsoever things are of good report; if there be any virtue, and if there be any praise, think on these things.
Philippians 4:6-8

**NOTHING IS EVER AS BAD
AS IT FIRST APPEARS.**
-MIKE MURDOCK

WORSHIP

Give unto the Lord the glory due unto His name: bring an offering, and come before Him: worship the Lord in the beauty of holiness.   *1 Chronicles 16:29*

It is a good thing to give thanks unto the Lord, and to sing praises unto Thy name, O most High: To shew forth Thy lovingkindness in the morning, and Thy faithfulness every night,   *Psalm 92:1,2*

I will extol Thee, my God, O king; and I will bless Thy name for ever and ever. Every day will I bless Thee; and I will praise Thy name for ever and ever. Great is the Lord, and greatly to be praised; and His greatness is unsearchable.
Psalm 145:1-3

And Jesus answered and said unto him, Get thee behind Me, satan: for it is written, Thou shalt worship the Lord thy God, and Him only shalt thou serve.
Luke 4:8

Now we know that God heareth not sinners: but if any man be a worshipper of God, and doeth His will, him He heareth.
John 9:31

TRUE WORSHIP IS NOT FORCED PASSION, IT IS AN UNAVOIDABLE INTIMACY. IT IS THE LOVE-ROOM WHERE YOUR FUTURE IS BORN.
-MIKE MURDOCK

31 FACTS ABOUT WISDOM

1. Wisdom Is The Master Key To All The Treasures Of Life. (2 Chronicles 1:7, 8,10-12; Colossians 2:2,3)

2. Wisdom Is A Gift From God To You. (Proverbs 2:6; Daniel 2:21; 1 Corinthians 12:8)

3. The Fear Of God Is The Beginning Of Wisdom. (Job 28:28; Psalm 111:10; Proverbs 9:10)

4. The Wisdom Of This World Is A False Substitute For The Wisdom Of God. (1 Corinthians 2:4,13; James 3:13-17)

5. The Wisdom Of Man Is Foolishness To God. (1 Corinthians 1:20, 21,25; 1 Corinthians 3:19)

6. Right Relationships Increase Your Wisdom. (Proverbs 13:20; 1 Corinthians 15:33; 2 Thessalonians 3:6; 1 Timothy 6:5)

7. The Wisdom Of God Is Foolishness To The Natural Mind. (Proverbs 18:2; Isaiah 55:8,9; 1 Corinthians 2:4,5)

8. Your Conversation Reveals How Much Wisdom You Possess. (1 Kings 10:24; Proverbs 18:21; Proverbs 29:11; James 3:2)

9. Jesus Is Made Unto Us Wisdom. (1 Corinthians 1:30; Ephesians 1:5,8,17)

10. All The Treasures Of Wisdom And Knowledge Are Hid In Jesus Christ. (1 Corinthians 1:23,24; 1 Corinthians 2:7,8; Colossians 2:2,3)

11. The Word Of God Is Your Source Of Wisdom. (Deuteronomy 4:5,6; Psalm 119:98-100; Proverbs 2:6)

12. God Will Give You Wisdom When You Take The Time To Listen. (Proverbs 2:6; Isaiah 40:31; John 10:27; James 1:5)

13. The Word Of God Is Able To Make You Wise Unto Salvation. (Psalm 107:43; John 5:39)

14. The Holy Spirit Is The Spirit Of Wisdom That Unleashes Your Gifts, Talents And Skills. (Exodus 31:1, 3,4; Exodus 36:1; Daniel 1:4)

15. Men Of Wisdom Will Always Be Men Of Mercy. (Galatians 6:1; James 3:17; James 5:19,20)

16. Wisdom Is Better Than Jewels Or Money. (Job 28:18; Proverbs 3:13-15; Proverbs 8:11; Proverbs 16:16)

17. Wisdom Is More Powerful Than Weapons Of War. (Proverbs 12:6; Ecclesiastes 9:18; Isaiah 33:6; Acts 6:10)

18. He That Wins Souls Is Wise. (Proverbs 11:30; Daniel 12:3; Romans 10:14,15)

19. The Wise Hate Evil And The Evil Hate The Wise. (Proverbs 1:7,22; Proverbs 8:13; Proverbs 9:8; Proverbs 18:2)

20. Wisdom Reveals The Treasure In Yourself. (Proverbs 19:8; Ephesians 2:10; Philippians 1:6; 1 Peter 2:9,10)

21. The Proof Of Wisdom Is The Presence Of Joy And Peace. (Psalm 119:165; Proverbs 3:13; Ecclesiastes 7:12; James 3:17)

22. Wisdom Makes Your Enemies Helpless Against You. (Proverbs 16:7; Ecclesiastes 7:12; Isaiah 54:17; Luke 21:15)

23. Wisdom Creates Currents Of Favor And Recognition Toward You. (Proverbs 3:1-4; Proverbs 4:8; Proverbs 8:34,35)

24. The Wise Welcome Correction. (Proverbs 3:11,12; Proverbs 9:8,9)
25. When The Wise Speak, Healing Flows. (Proverbs 10:11,20,21; Proverbs 12:18)
26. When You Increase Your Wisdom You Will Increase Your Wealth. (Psalm 112:1-3; Proverbs 3:16; Proverbs 8:18-21; Proverbs 14:24)
27. Wisdom Can Be Imparted By The Laying On Of Hands Of A Man Of God. (Deuteronomy 34:9; Acts 6:6-8,10; 2 Timothy 1:6,14)
28. Wisdom Guarantees Promotion. (Proverbs 4:8,9; Proverbs 8:15,16; Ezra 7:25)
29. Wisdom Loves Those Who Love Her. (Proverbs 2:3-5; Proverbs 8:17,21)
30. Wisdom Will Be Given To You When You Pray For It In Faith. (Matthew 7:7,8,11; James 1:5,6)
31. The Mantle Of Wisdom Makes You Ten Times Stronger Than Those Without It. (Psalm 91:7; Ecclesiastes 7:19; Daniel 1:17,20)

101 WISDOM KEYS

1. Never Complain About What You Permit.
2. The Problem That Infuriates You The Most Is The Problem That God Has Assigned You To Solve.
3. Those Who Unlock Your Compassion Are Those To Whom You Have Been Assigned.
4. What You Are Willing To Walk Away From Determines What God Will Bring To You.
5. The Secret Of Your Future Is Hidden In Your Daily Routine.
6. Your Rewards In Life Are Determined By The Problems You Solve For Others.
7. When You Want Something You Have Never Had, You Have Got To Do Something You Have Never Done.
8. All Men Fall...The Great Ones Get Back Up.
9. Intolerance Of Your Present Creates Your Future.
10. Those Who Cannot Increase You Will Inevitably Decrease You.
11. You Will Never Leave Where

You Are Until You Decide Where
You Would Rather Be.

12. You Will Only Have Significant
    Success With Something That Is
    An Obsession.

13. Give Another What He Cannot
    Find Anywhere Else And He
    Will Keep Returning.

14. Your Assignment Is Not Your
    Decision But Your Discovery.

15. When Fatigue Walks In, Faith
    Walks Out.

16. If What You Hold In Your Hand
    Is Not Enough To Be Your
    Harvest, Make It Your Seed.

17. You Will Never Change What
    You Believe Until Your Belief
    System Cannot Produce
    Something You Want.

18. You Will Only Be Pursued For
    The Problems You Solve.

19. Champions Are Willing To Do
    Things They Hate To Create
    Something They Love.

20. You Will Never Possess What
    You Are Unwilling To Pursue.

21. The Only Reason Men Fail Is
    Broken Focus.

22. Stop Looking At Where You
    Have Been And Start Looking
    At Where You Can Be.

23. You Will Only Be Remembered For Two Things; The Problems You Solve Or The Ones You Create.
24. Those Who Transfer Knowledge Are Also Capable Of Transferring Error.
25. Your Seed Is The Only Influence You Have Over Your Future.
26. Loneliness Is Not The Absence Of Affection, But The Absence Of Direction.
27. You Cannot Be What You Are Not, But You Can Become What You Are Not.
28. False Accusation Is The Last Stage Before Supernatural Promotion.
29. Your Seed Is A Photograph Of Your Faith.
30. What You Repeatedly Hear You Will Eventually Believe.
31. God Never Consults Your Past To Determine Your Future.
32. Satan Always Attacks Those Next In Line For A Promotion.
33. Power Is The Ability To Walk Away From Something You Desire...To Protect Something You Love.
34. Anything That Does Not

Change You Is Unnecessary In Your Life.

35. When You Discover Your Assignment, You Will Discover Your Enemy.

36. What You Respect, You Will Attract.

37. Men Decide Their Habits...Their Habits Decide Their Future.

38. You Cannot Correct What You Are Unwilling To Confront.

39. The Proof Of Desire Is Pursuit.

40. Crisis Always Occurs At The Curve Of Change.

41. If Time Heals, God Is Unnecessary.

42. Your Seed Is Anything That Benefits Another While Your Harvest Is Anything That Benefits You.

43. Satan's Favorite Entry Point Into Your Life Is Always Through Someone Close To You.

44. What You Hate Reveals What You Were Created To Correct.

45. Losers Focus On What They Are Going Through While Champions Focus On What They Are Going To.

46. When You Let Go Of What Is In Your Hand, God Will Let Go Of

What Is In His Hand.

47. Pain Is Not An Enemy But Merely The Proof That One Exists.

48. When God Wants To Bless You, He Puts A Person In Your Life... When Satan Wants To Destroy You, He Puts A Person In Your Life.

49. Currents Of Favor Begin To Flow The Moment You Solve A Problem For Someone.

50. The Seed That Leaves Your Hand Never Leaves Your Life...But Enters Your Future, Where It Multiplies.

51. Each Act Of Obedience Shortens The Distance To Any Miracle You Are Pursuing.

52. The Quality Of Your Preparation Determines The Quality Of Your Performance.

53. Champions Make Decisions That Create The Future They Desire...Losers Make Decisions That Create The Present They Desire.

54. Creativity Is The Search For Options; Concentration Is The Elimination Of Them.

55. Seed-Faith Is Sowing What You Have Been Given...To Create

What You Have Been Promised.

56. The Seasons Of Your Life Will Change Every Time You Decide To Use Your Faith.

57. Someone Is Always Observing You Who Is Capable Of Greatly Blessing You.

58. Giving Is Proof That You Have Conquered Greed.

59. The Season For Research Is Not TheSeason For Marketing.

60. What You Fail To Master In Your Life Will Eventually Master You.

61. Go Where You Are Celebrated Instead Of Where You Are Tolerated.

62. The Broken Become Masters At Mending.

63. Your Significance Is Not In Your Similarity To Another, But In Your Point Of Difference From Another.

64. You Will Always Pursue The Friendship That Solves Your Most Immediate Problem.

65. The Worth Of Any Relationship Can Be Measured By Its Contributions To Your Priorities.

66. You Will Never Conquer What You Refuse To Hate.

67. Injustice Is Only As Powerful As Your Memory Of It.
68. Every Relationship In Your Life Is A Current Moving You Toward Your Dreams Or Away From Them.
69. You Will Never Be Promoted Until You Have Become Over-Qualified For Your Present Assignment.
70. Money Is Merely A Reward For Solving Problems.
71. Your Reaction To Someone In Trouble Determines God's Reaction To You The Next Time You Get In Trouble.
72. What You Can Tolerate, You Cannot Change.
73. The Waves Of Yesterday's Disobedience Will Splash On The Shores Of Today For A Season.
74. You Will Never Outgrow Warfare...You Must Simply Learn To Fight.
75. Nothing Is Ever As Bad As it First Appears.
76. The Evidence Of God's Presence Far Outweighs The Proof Of His Absence.
77. Patience Is The Weapon That

Forces Deception To Reveal
Itself.
78. One Hour In The Presence Of
God Will Reveal Any Flaw In
Your Most Carefully Laid Plan.
79. Never Spend More Time On A
Critic Than You Would Give To
A Friend.
80. Those Who Do Not Respect Your
Assignment Disqualify
Themselves For A Relationship.
81. You Will Never Reach The
Palace Talking Like A
Peasant.
82. Struggle Is The Proof You Have
Not Yet Been Conquered.
83. Never Discuss Your Problem
With Someone Incapable Of
Solving It.
84. Greatness Is Not The Pursuit Of
Perfection But The Pursuit Of
Completion.
85. Never Rewrite Your Theology To
Accommodate A Tragedy.
86. The Greatest Quality On Earth
Is The Willingness To Become.
87. Warfare Always Surrounds The
Birth Of A Miracle.
88. Failure Is Not An Event, But An
Opinion.
89. You Are Never As Far From A

Miracle As It First Appears.
90. What You See Determines What You Desire.
91. The Atmosphere You Permit Determines The Product You Produce.
92. Prosperity Is Simply Having Enough Of God's Provision To Complete His Instructions For Your Life.
93. God Will Never Advance Your Instructions Beyond Your Last Act Of Disobedience.
94. Anger Is The Birthplace For Solutions.
95. Those Who Do Not Respect Your Time Will Not Respect Your Wisdom Either.
96. Discontent Is The Catalyst For Change.
97. Crisis Is Merely Concentrated Information.
98. Silence Cannot Be Misquoted.
99. Those Who Created The Pain Of Yesterday Do Not Control The Pleasure Of Tomorrow.
100. When You Change Your Focus You Will Change Your Feelings.
101. What You Make Happen For Others, God Will Make Happen For You.

31 FACTS ABOUT FAVOR

1. Uncommon Favor Is When God Causes Someone To Desire To Become A Problem Solver In Your Life. (Ruth 2:8-12)
2. Uncommon Favor Is A Gift From God That Can Stop If It Is Not Recognized And Celebrated. (Revelation 3:7)
3. Uncommon Favor Is Only Guaranteed To Those Who Qualify Through Acts Of Obedience. (Deuteronomy 28:1,2)
4. Uncommon Success Will Require Uncommon Favor From Someone. (Deuteronomy 16:15)
5. Uncommon Favor Is An Attitude Of Goodness Toward You, Not An Exchange Or Payment For Something You Have Done. (Ruth 2:8-12)
6. Uncommon Favor Is An Exception To The Rule, Not A Normality. (Psalm 127:1)
7. Uncommon Favor Must Begin As A Seed From You Before It Returns As A Harvest To You. (Galatians 6:7)

8. When You Sow Seeds Of Favor Consistently, You Will Reap The Harvest Of Favor Consistently. (Galatians 6:7,8)

9. The Seed Of Uncommon Favor Can Grow Over A Period Of Time. (Luke 2:52)

10. Uncommon Favor Can Make You Wealthy In A Single Day. (Ruth 4:13)

11. Uncommon Favor Can Silence A Lifetime Enemy Forever. (Esther 3:5; 7:9-10)

12. Uncommon Favor Can Make You A Household Name In 24 Hours. (Esther 2:16)

13. Uncommon Favor Can Double Your Financial Worth In The Midst Of Your Worst Tragedy. (Job 42:10-12)

14. Uncommon Favor Can Accelerate The Timetable Of Your Assignment And Destiny. (Genesis 41:39-43)

15. One Day Of Favor Is Worth A Lifetime Of Labor. (Ruth 4:10)

16. Uncommon Favor Comes When Uncommon Intercessors Pray For You. (Acts 12:5)

17. Uncommon Favor Always Begins When You Solve An

Uncommon Problem For
Someone. (Genesis 41:42-44)
18. Currents Of Favor Always Flow
When You Solve The Problem
Nearest You. (Genesis 40:4-8)
19. Uncommon Favor Will Usually
Come Through Someone
Observing You Who Is Capable
Of Greatly Blessing You. (Ruth
2:8,9)
20. Uncommon Favor Is Not An
Accident, But A Deliberate
Design By God To Reward You
For Acts Of Obedience Invisible
To Others. (Isaiah 1:19)
21. Uncommon Favor Will Stop
When You Deliberately Ignore
An Instruction From God.
(1 Samuel 15:9-11,26)
22. The Flow Of Uncommon Favor
Is Often Paralyzed Through The
Development Of Arrogance And
Self-Sufficiency. (Daniel 5:20,
21)
23. Uncommon Favor Can Stop A
Tragedy Instantly In Your Life.
(Genesis 41:39,40)
24. The River Of Uncommon Favor
Will Dry Up When God
Observes Greed. (Malachi 3:8,9)

25. Uncommon Favor Is A Seed That Anyone Can Sow Into The Life Of Another. (Ruth 2:8,9)

26. Uncommon Favor Should Be Pursued, Requested And Celebrated. (Esther 5:1-4)

27. Uncommon Favor Is Often The Only Exit From A Place Of Captivity And Bondage. (Genesis 40:14)

28. Uncommon Favor Will Cease When Not Received With Thankfulness. (Matthew 18:21-35)

29. Honoring Your Parents Is The First Clue In Understanding The Law Of Favor. (Exodus 20:12)

30. Uncommon Men Always Sow Favor. (Ruth 2:8,9)

31. The Favor Of God Will Always Create Favor With Men. (Luke 2:52)

31 FACTS ABOUT THE UNCOMMON FATHER

1. The Uncommon Father Highly Esteems The Word Of God. (Psalm 119:89; Matthew 24:35)
2. The Uncommon Father Teaches His Children To Pray. (1 Samuel 12:23)
3. The Uncommon Father Refuses To Focus On Mistakes. (Isaiah 43,13,19)
4. The Uncommon Father Is Willing To Change His Opinion. (Isaiah 43:19)
5. The Uncommon Father Mentors His Children On The Power Of Forgiveness. (Ephesians 4:32)
6. The Uncommon Father Avoids Unnecessary Confrontation. (Romans 12:18)
7. The Uncommon Father Knows His Seeds Of Patience Will Grow Greatness In His Children. (Psalm 37:7)
8. The Uncommon Father Chooses

His Words Carefully. (Proverbs 17:27,28)

9. The Uncommon Father Rejoices When His Children Achieve Their Goals. (Romans 12:15)

10. The Uncommon Father Leaves An Uncommon Legacy For His Children. (Proverbs 13:22)

11. The Uncommon Father Praises Quickly And Criticizes Slowly. (Proverbs 18:21)

12. The Uncommon Father Is An Uncommon Listener. (Proverbs 20:12)

13. The Uncommon Father Withholds His Judgment Until All The Facts Are Known. (Romans 2:1)

14. The Uncommon Father Seeks To Know His Children Well. (Psalm 127:3,4)

15. The Uncommon Father Is A Harbor, Not A Storm. (2 Timothy 2:24)

16. The Uncommon Father Lavishes Affection, Love And Approval On His Children. (Romans 12:10)

17. The Uncommon Father Will Not

Permit Disrespect From His
Children. (Proverbs 22:6)

18. The Uncommon Father Con-
tinually Evaluates The Friends
His Children Choose.
(Ephesians 5:11)

19. The Uncommon Father Mentors
His Children On The Danger Of
Uncontrolled Anger. (Ephesians
4:26,27)

20. The Uncommon Father Is
Unafraid To Pursue Personal
Counseling. (Proverbs 11:14)

21. The Uncommon Father Never
Quits Believing In His Children.
(James 1:12)

22. The Uncommon Father Pursues
Spiritual Mentorship.
(Hebrews 10:25)

23. The Uncommon Father Will Not
Permit Strife In His House.
(Proverbs 15:1)

24. The Uncommon Father Refuses
To Grieve And Offend The Holy
Spirit. (Ephesians 4:29,30)

25. The Uncommon Father Always
Tells The Truth. *Always.*
(Romans 23:17)

26. The Uncommon Father Is

Always Accessible To His
Children. (Jeremiah 33:3)

27. The Uncommon Father Teaches
His Children To Respect Money.
(Ecclesiastes 10:19)

28. The Uncommon Father Prays
For His Children Daily.
(1 Samuel 12:23)

29. The Uncommon Father Is
Concerned About The Quality
Of Man His Daughter Chooses
To Marry. (2 Corinthians 2:11)

30. The Uncommon Father Is The
Personal Success Coach Of His
Family. (Proverbs 13:1; Proverbs
29:17)

31. The Uncommon Father Sows
Wisdom Continuously Into The
Hearts Of His Children.
(Proverbs 4:7)

58 LEADERSHIP SECRETS OF JESUS

1. Jesus Was A Problem-Solver. (Acts 10:38)
2. Jesus Believed In His Product. (John 4:13,14)
3. Jesus Never Misrepresented His Product. (Matthew 8:20)
4. Jesus Went Where The People Were. (Luke 9:6)
5. Jesus Took Time To Rest. (Mark 6:31)
6. Jesus Took Time To Plan. (John 14:2)
7. Jesus Knew He Did Not Have To Close Every Sale To Be A Success. (John 1:11,12)
8. Jesus Had Something Others Needed. (Luke 6:19)
9. Jesus Was Concerned About The Finances Of People. (Mark 10:29,30; Luke 5:1-11)
10. Jesus Was Willing To Go Where He Had Never Been Before. (Matthew 8:5,28)
11. Jesus Never Allowed What

Others Said About Him To
Change His Opinion Of Himself.
(Luke 6:22,23)

12. Jesus Understood Timing And
Preparation. (John 2:4)

13. Jesus Developed A Passion For
His Goals. (Luke 19:10)

14. Jesus Respected Authority.
(Mark 12:17)

15. Jesus Never Discriminated.
(Acts 10:34)

16. Jesus Offered Incentives. (John
14:2)

17. Jesus Overcame The Stigma Of
A Questionable Background.
(Matthew 1:20)

18. Jesus Never Wasted Time
Answering Critics. (Matthew
26:63)

19. Jesus Knew There Was A Right
Time And A Wrong Time To
Approach People. (John 8:11)

20. Jesus Educated Those He
Mentored. (Luke 13:10;
Mark 6:6)

21. Jesus Refused To Be
Discouraged When Others
Misjudge His Motives.
(Matthew 12:24)

22. Jesus Refused To Be Bitter When Others Were Disloyal Or Betrayed Him. (Mark 14:18)

23. Jesus Networked With People Of All Backgrounds. (Luke 5:1-4; Luke 19:5-10)

24. Jesus Resisted Temptation. (Matthew 4:1-11)

25. Jesus Made Decisions That Created A Desired Future Instead Of A Desired Present. (Luke 23:33,46)

26. Jesus Never Judged People By Their Outward Appearance. (John 4:39)

27. Jesus Recognized The Law Of Repetition. (John 8:12)

28. Jesus Was A Tomorrow Thinker. (John 8:11)

29. Jesus Knew That Money Alone Could Not Bring Contentment. (Luke 18:18-25)

30. Jesus Knew The Power Of Words And The Power Of Silence. (Luke 6:45; Matthew 12:36,37)

31. Jesus Knew When You Want Something You Have Never Had, You Have To Do Something

You Have Never Done.
(Matthew 14:29)

32. Jesus Permitted Others To Correct Their Mistakes. (John 4:7-30)

33. Jesus Knew His Worth. (Luke 7:44-46)

34. Jesus Never Tried To Succeed Alone. (John 5:30)

35. Jesus Knew That Money Is Anywhere You Really Want It To Be. (Matthew 17:27)

36. Jesus Set Specific Goals. (Luke 19:10)

37. Jesus Knew That Every Great Achievement Requires A Willingness To Begin Small. (John 1:45,46)

38. Jesus Hurt When Others Hurt. (Matthew 14:14)

39. Jesus Was Not Afraid To Show His Feelings. (John 2:14,15)

40. Jesus Knew The Power Of Habit. (Luke 4:16)

41. Jesus Finished What He Started. (John 19:30)

42. Jesus Was Knowledgeable Of Scripture. (Luke 4)

43. Jesus Never Hurried. (John 11:1-44)

44. Jesus Went Where He Was Celebrated Instead Of Where He Was Tolerated. (Matthew 10:14)

45. Jesus Constantly Consulted His Heavenly Father. (John 5:19; Matthew 26:39,42)

46. Jesus Knew That Prayer Generated Results. (Matthew 26:44)

47. Jesus Rose Early. (Mark 1:35)

48. Jesus Never Felt He Had To Prove Himself To Anyone. (Matthew 4:3,4)

49. Jesus Avoided Unnecessary Confrontations. (Luke 4:29,30)

50. Jesus Delegated. (Matthew 14:19)

51. Jesus Carefully Guarded His Personal Schedule. (John 11:6)

52. Jesus Asked Questions To Accurately Determine The Needs And Desires Of Others. (John 21:5)

53. Jesus Always Answered Truthfully. (John 14:6)

54. Jesus Stayed In The Center Of His Expertise. (Acts 10:38)

55. Jesus Accepted The Responsibility For The Mistakes Of Those

Under His Authority. (Luke 22:31,32)

56. Jesus Pursued The Mentorship Of More Experienced Men. (Luke 2:46)

57. Jesus Did Not Permit Those He Led To Show Disrespect. (Matthew 16:22)

58. Jesus Respected The Law Of Sowing And Reaping. (Luke 6:38)

DECISION PAGE

Will You Accept Jesus As Your Personal Savior Today?

The Bible says, "That if thou shalt confess with thy mouth the Lord Jesus, and shalt believe in thine heart that God hath raised Him from the dead, thou shalt be saved" (Romans 10:9).

Pray this prayer from your heart today!

"Dear Jesus, I believe that You died for me and rose again on the third day. I confess that I am a sinner...I need Your love and forgiveness. Come into my heart. Forgive my sins. I receive Your eternal life. Confirm Your love by giving me peace, joy and supernatural love for others. Amen."

Return this today!

☐ Yes, Mike! I made a decision to accept Christ as my personal Savior today. Please send me my free gift of your book, *"31 Keys To A New Beginning"* to help me with my new life in Christ. *(B-48)*

Clip and Mail

NAME	BIRTHDAY

ADDRESS		
CITY	STATE	ZIP
PHONE	E-MAIL	*B-51*

Mail form to:

The Wisdom Center
P.O. Box 99 · Denton, Texas 76202
1-888-WISDOM-1 (1-888-947-3661)
Website: www.thewisdomcenter.tv

ABOUT *MIKE MURDOCK*

- Has embraced his Assignment to pursue... proclaim...and publish the Wisdom of God to help people achieve their dreams and goals.

- Began full-time evangelism at the age of 19, which has continued since 1966.

- Has traveled and spoken to more than 14,000 audiences in 38 countries, including East and West Africa, the Orient and Europe.

- Noted author of 130 books, including best sellers, *"Wisdom For Winning," "Dream Seeds"* and *"The Double Diamond Principle."*

- Created the popular *"Topical Bible"* series for Businessmen, Mothers, Fathers, Teenagers; *"The One-Minute Pocket Bible"* series, and *"The Uncommon Life"* series.

- Has composed more than 5,700 songs such as *"I Am Blessed," "You Can Make It," "God Rides On Wings Of Love"* and *"Jesus, Just The Mention Of Your Name,"* recorded by many gospel artists.

- Is the Founder of The Wisdom Center, in Denton, Texas.

- Has a weekly television program called *"Wisdom Keys With Mike Murdock."*

- Has appeared often on TBN, CBN, BET and other television network programs.

- Is a Founding Trustee on the Board of International Charismatic Bible Ministries with Oral Roberts.

- Has had more than 3,500 accept the call into full-time ministry under his ministry.

Personal Notes

Personal Notes

